The School As A Home
For The Mind

The School As A Home For The Mind

————— ❦ —————

A collection of articles by
Arthur L. Costa

Skylight Publishing
Palatine, Illinois

The School As A Home For The Mind
Second Printing

Published by Skylight Publishing, Inc.
200 East Wood Street, Suite 274
Palatine, Illinois 60067
1-800-348-4474 (in northern Illinois 1-708-991-6300)
FAX 1-708-991-6420

Senior Editor: Robin Fogarty
Production Editor: Julia E. Noblitt
Book and Cover Design: David Stockman
Type Composer: Donna Ramirez
Production Coordinator: Ari Ohlson
Indexer: Schroeder Indexing Services

Printed in the United States of America
Library of Congress Catalog Card Number 91-61609
ISBN 0-932935-33-8

ARTHUR L. COSTA

A leading proponent of the explicit teaching of thinking throughout every school curriculum, Art is known for enriching the lives of children throughout the world. Throughout his long and distinguished career, he has created a compelling vision of how and why educators need to consciously instill thoughtfulness into all schools. He has shown teachers how to translate the research on thinking into enjoyable classroom activities, and guided administrators into new roles as instructional leaders who create school climates conducive to thinking.

As a teacher, visiting professor, workshop presenter, and consultant, Art has worked in all fifty states and U.S. territories, as well as in numerous countries abroad, including Austria, Canada, Fiji, France, Korea, Micronesia, Mexico, the Philippines, Spain, West Germany, and Zaire.

An educator since the mid-1950s, when he first began teaching seventh and eighth graders in Bellflower, California, Art received his master's degree in 1958 and doctorate in 1969 from the University of Southern California.

Art is the author and co-author of numerous books, including *Investigating Science with Children, Enabling Behaviors, Basic Teacher Behaviors, Supervision for Intelligent Teaching, Strategies for Science Teaching,* and *Communication Skills.* He is also a contributor to collections of educational research, including *Using What We Know About Teaching* and *Perspectives on Effective Teaching and the Cooperative Classroom.* In addition to writing for education journals such as *Educational Leadership,* Art also served as editor of both the first and second editions of the best-selling ASCD resource book on the teaching of thinking, *Developing Minds.* He is co-director of the Institute for Intelligent Behavior.

Long recognized for his unique talent and dedication to teachers, children, and education, Art is the recipient of numerous appointments and awards. His long record of service includes a term as 1988-1989 president of the Association for Supervision and Curriculum Development (ASCD), a Distinguished Service Award in 1983 for his work on "Project Leadership" with the Association of California School Administrators, and participation in the Select Curriculum Committee of ASCD, 1981-84.

In 1991 he celebrates his retirement as a professor of Educational Administration at California State University, Sacramento. Following his retirement, Art will live in Hawaii with his wife, Nancy, and continue his consulting worldwide. He remains dedicated to helping educators make schools exciting, challenging places which can truly be called "homes for the mind."

Table of Contents

Introduction

The Costa Collection begins with his seminal piece, "The School As A Home For The Mind." His opening statement, "A quiet revolution is taking place across America in corporate offices, industrial factories, government offices—and in schools as well. It is a revolution of the intellect, placing a premium on our greatest natural resource, the human mind," sets the stage for his elaboration on the school as a home for the mind. Throughout this collection, Costa spells out this "revolution of the intellect" that is reshaping our schools.

The articles, ranging from visionary images to point-specific procedures for attaining that vision, cluster into several arenas. The groupings contain original articles that reveal Costa's best thinking on key questions evoked by the idea of a "revolution of the intellect":

What is the vision of this "intellectual revolution"?

How do we teach to the intellect?

What are the roles of the key players?

How do we assess what we're doing?

How do we restructure the school as a home for the mind?

School As A Home For The Mind: The Vision

The opening group of articles presents Costa's visionary portrait of the future school. The notion of "Aesthetics: Where Thinking Originates" suggests that cognition (with the addition of aesthetics) shifts from mere passive comprehension to a tenacious quest in which "children...reflect on the...beauty in a sunset, intrigue in the geometrics of a spider web, and exhilaration in the iridescence of a hummingbird's wings." In these beginning pieces, Costa also outlines his well-known and often-quoted list of intelligent behaviors: persistence, decreased impulsivity, empathic listening, cooperative thinking, flexible thinking, metacognition, checking for accuracy, drawing on past knowledge and applying it to new situations, question and problem posing, risk taking, a sense of humor, precision of language, use of all senses, ingenuity, and a sense of efficacy as a thinker.

The Thoughtful Curriculum

Supporting the vision presented in Section I, the second cluster of articles delineates how to teach to the intellect. Costa defines Brandt's framework of teaching **for, of** and **about** thinking as a universal organizer for the thoughtful classroom. In his exquisite elaboration on setting the climate **for** thinking, Costa develops the notion of questioning strategies that elicit student thinking and learning. He uses the "Three-Story Intellect" model in which the language of the classroom is designed to gather information, make sense of that information, and apply it in novel situations.

The companion piece to "Teacher-Initiated Questions And Directions That Elicit Thinking And Learning" is Costa's article on response behaviors, "Teacher Response Behaviors That Support And Extend Thinking And Learning." To further set the climate and conditions for thoughtfulness in the classroom, Costa discusses six responses that include terminal or closed teacher response strategies and open and extending response techniques.

In developing the second component of the thoughtful classroom, teaching the skills **of** thinking, Costa suggests that thinking skills are neither an add-on nor a quick fix, but rather a total rededication of the basic value system of the school as an intellectually stimulating place. In addition to recognizing the value of teaching the skills of thinking, a description of how to teach thinking skills explicitly is directly related to the Three-Story Intellect model of thoughtful classroom instruction.

Finally, to complete this cluster of articles on how to teach the skills of thoughtfulness, "Mediating The Metacognitive" highlights a dozen mediation strategies to help teach **about** thinking.

Costa explains, "If you [have an] 'inner' dialogue inside your brain, and if you...stop to evaluate your own decision-making/problem-solving processes, you [are] experiencing metacognition." It is in this "thinking about thinking" mode that students learn about their own thinking.

This section of articles presents myriad practical ideas and instructional strategies. It is a synthesis of "how-tos" for the thoughtful classroom.

The Key Players

Beyond the curricular focus of teaching for, of, and about thinking, Costa's third cluster of articles focuses on the key players in this "revolution of the intellect" in creating the school as a home for the mind. He examines the question of "What goes on in your head when you teach?" from the supervisory perspective, or as a planning stage to the teaching act.

In addition, he asks, "Do you speak Cogitare?" and proceeds with a plea to teachers to monitor their teaching for use of specific cognitive terminology. By asking questions, selecting terms, clarifying ideas and processes, providing data, and withholding value judgments, we can stimulate and enhance the intelligence of others to complete the teaching cycle. Section III also includes an article on cognitive coaching as a reflective strategy for teachers to look back and evaluate their own teaching.

The final article in this section presents a discussion of an often-asked question: what is the administrator's role in enhancing thinking skills? This article offers suggestions on how principals can exert influence in enhancing students' full intellect. Ideas presented for administrators to consider include ways to create conditions, use available resources, and model practices.

The Evaluation Dilemma

Addressing the critical issue of assessment of the intellectual functions promoted in the thoughtful classroom, this fourth cluster of articles contains two distinct pieces. The first piece addresses the dilemma created by trying to test "thinking [that] is in a dynamic state of flux...[with] norm-referenced, standardized test scores...[which] provide us with a more static number reflecting the achievement and performance of isolated skills." His classic question, "Is testing thinking an oxymoron?" signals the assessment dilemma caused by this revolution of the intellect.

In another article in this section, Costa again delineates the dispositions of intelligent behavior that seem to be worthy indicators for assessing the growing intelligence of our students. Along with the questions posed in the assessment piece, Costa asks the more

encompassing evaluation question: "Has thinking been infused into the entire school culture?" Here he develops a list of global indicators for school-wide evaluation. Included among the indicators are evidence of collegiality, experimentation and action research, appreciation and recognition, high expectations, priority protection, tangible support, celebration, communication, trust, and modeling.

The School As A Home For The Mind: The Re-vision

Costa summarizes his vision in a concluding statement:

> The school will become a home for the mind only when the total school is an intellectually stimulating environment for all participants; when all the school's inhabitants realize that freeing human intellectual potential is the goal of education; when they strive to get better at it themselves; and when they use their energies to enhance the intelligent behavior of others.

To re-visit that belief, the school as a home for the mind, his final article describes the orchestration necessary to realize the vision.

In the restructuring process that results from the "revolution of the intellect," Costa suggests seven phases: definition, integration, application, articulation, individualization, politicization, and evaluation. He likens the orchestration of the musician's world to that of the school:

> In an orchestra,...musicians play in the same key, and at the same tempo. They rehearse together and have a common vision of the entire score, each knowing well the part they play that contributes to the whole. They do not all play at the same time; there are rests, harmonies, fugues, and counterpoint. They support each other in a totally coordinated and concerted effort. In the same way, teachers can support each other in creating an overall curriculum. They neither teach the same thinking processes at the same time, nor do they approach them in the same way. Their cumulative effect, however, is beautiful, harmonious 'music' in the mind and the learning of the student.

This then is what the revolution is about—this revolution of the intellect in which the school is a home for the mind.

Robin Fogarty
Editor

Section I

The School As A Home For The Mind: The Vision

"In a school that is a home for the mind there is an inherent faith that all people can continue to improve their intellectual capacities throughout life; that learning to think is as valid a goal for the 'at risk,' handicapped, the disadvantaged, and the foreign-speaking as it is for the 'gifted and talented,' and that all of us have the potential for even greater creativity and intellectual power."

—*Arthur L. Costa*

The School As A Home For The Mind

A quiet revolution is taking place across America in corporate offices, industrial factories, government offices—and in schools as well. It is a revolution of the intellect, placing a premium on our greatest natural resource, the human mind. Increasingly, those attributes of a climate conducive to intellectual growth and self-fulfillment are becoming universally recognized and accepted. The conditions that maximize creativity are being described, understood, and replicated (Perkins 1983, Kohn 1987, Deal 1987, Boyer 1988, McClure 1988, Saphier 1987). The new paradigm of industrial management emphasizes an environment in which growth and empowerment of the individual are the keys to corporate success. Pascarella writes in *The New Achievers* (1984):

> Management is heading toward a new state of mind—a new perception of its own role and that of the organization. It is slowly moving from seeking power to empowering others, from controlling people to enabling them to be creative.... As managers make a fundamental shift in values...the corporation undergoes a radical reorientation to a greater world view.

Many educators have advocated similar school conditions for years, believing that a climate which maximizes human potential can be developed, monitored, and sustained. These conditions are equally applicable at all levels of the educational organization: classrooms, schools, and school districts.

Shaping Teachers' Thinking

Many factors influence teachers' thinking as they make decisions about curriculum, instruction, and content. Their own cultural background, cognitive style, and professional values and beliefs about education all subconsciously enter their daily decision making. Knowledge of students' needs

1

and perceptions of students' abilities and backgrounds influence teacher judgments about when to teach what to whom. The available resources for instruction—tests, materials, equipment, textbooks, and time and space—all have an impact on teachers' instructional planning.

Less obvious influences on teacher thought, but vastly more compelling, are the norms, culture, and climate of the school setting. Hidden but powerful cues emanate from the school environment. They signal the institutional value system that governs the operation of the organization (Saphier and King 1985). Similarly, classroom cues signal a hidden, implicit curriculum that influences student thinking as well.

Recent efforts to bring an intellectual focus to our schools most likely will prove futile unless we create a school environment that signals the staff, students, and community that development of the intellect is of prime importance as the school's goal. While efforts to enhance the staff's instructional competencies, develop curriculum, revise instructional materials and testing procedures, and pilot and adopt published programs are important components in implementing cognitive education, it is crucial that the school climate in which teachers make their decisions be aligned with the goals of full intellectual development.

Unfortunately, schools can be intellectually depressing, not only for

students but for teachers as well. John Goodlad (1984) found that:

- Teachers are extremely isolated. They perform their craft behind closed doors and have little time within rigid daily schedules to meet, plan, observe, and talk with each other.

- Teachers often lack a sense of power and efficacy. Some feel they are at the bottom of hierarchy while the decisions and evaluations affecting them are being made "up there" someplace.

- The complex, intelligent act of teaching is often reduced to formulas or series of steps and competencies, the uniform performance of which supposedly connotes excellence in the art and elegance of teaching.

- Information about student achievement is for political, evaluative, or coercive purposes; it neither involves nor instructs the school staff members in reflecting on, evaluating, and improving curriculum and instruction.

- Educational innovations are often viewed as mere "tinkering" with the instructional program. There are so many of them, and their impact is so limited, that teachers sometimes feel, "If I do nothing, this, too, shall pass." Instead of institutionalizing change, traditional practices and policies so deeply entrenched in the educational bureaucracy remain static. Testing, reporting, securing parent understanding and support, teacher evaluation, scheduling, school organization, and discipline procedures are seldom revised to harmonize with the overall innovation.

When such a dismal school climate exists, teachers understandably become depressed. Their vivid imagination, altruism, creativity, and intellectual prowess may soon succumb to the humdrum dailiness of unruly students, irrelevant curriculum, impersonal surroundings, and equally disinterested co-workers. Under such conditions, the likelihood that teachers will value the development of students' intellect is marginal.

Toward The School As A Home For The Mind

Teachers are more likely to teach for thinking in an intellectually stimulating environment. When the conditions in which teachers work signal, promote, and facilitate their intellectual growth, they will gradually align their classrooms and instruction to promote students' intellectual growth as well. As teachers teach students to think, become more aware of conditions that promote student thinking, and become more powerful thinkers themselves, they will demand and create school climate conditions that are intellectually growth-producing as well. Thus, respect for intelligent behavior grows to pervade all levels of the institution.

Three climate conditions, in particular, facilitate intellectual growth: (1) all participants share a common vision of the school as a home for the mind, (2) the process of thinking is the content of curriculum and instruction, and (3) schools and classrooms are interdependent communities. These conditions provide a sharper image of a climate for thinking in schools and classrooms that are dedicated to becoming homes for the mind.

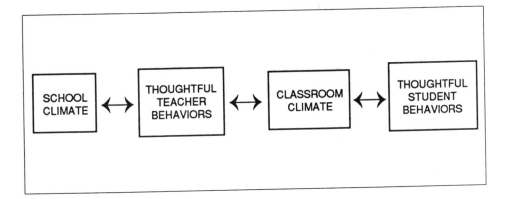

A Common Vision

Effective organizations are characterized by a deep sense of purposefulness and a vision of the future. Members at all levels share a commitment to that vision, a sense of ownership, and an internal responsibility for performance (Harmon 1988). This shared vision is evident in several ways.

Faith in Human Intellectual Potential

In a school that is a home for the mind there is an inherent faith that all people can continue to improve their intellectual capacities throughout life; that learning to think is as valid a goal for the "at-risk," the handicapped, the disadvantaged, and the foreign-speaking as it is for the "gifted and talented;" and that all of us have the potential for even greater creativity and intellectual power. Students, teachers, and administrators realize that learning to use and continually refine their intelligent behavior is the purpose of their life-long education. Such a belief is expressed in many ways.

Thinking is valued not only for all students and certificated staff, but for the classified staff as well. A principal of a "thinking school" in Davis, California, reported that a newly hired custodian constantly asked her to check on how well he was cleaning the classrooms and to tell him whether he was doing an adequate job. She decided to help him develop a clear mental image of what a clean class-room looked like and then worked to enhance his ability to evaluate for himself how well the room he cleaned fit that image.

School staff members continue to define and clarify thinking as a goal and seek ways to gain assistance in achieving it. Their commitment is reinforced when they are able to report and share progress toward installing thinking in their schools and classrooms. The superintendent of Manheim Township in Lancaster, Pennsylvania, reviews with site administrators their long-range goals and progress toward including the development of intelligent behaviors in the school's mission. In classrooms in Wayzata, Minnesota, students keep journals and periodically report new insights about their own creative problem-solving strategies.

Philosophy, Policies, and Practices

The vision is also expressed in the district's board-adopted mission statement, purposes, and policies. In Hopkins, Minnesota, enhancing intelligent behavior is explicitly stated in the school district's adopted philosophy and mission. District policies and practices are constantly scrutinized for their consistency with and contribution to that philosophy. Evidence of their use as criteria for decision making is examined. Furthermore, procedures for continuing to study, refine, and improve district-wide practices encourage schools to keep growing toward more thoughtful practice.

Personnel practices, for example, reflect the desire to infuse thinking. Job specifications for hiring new personnel include skills in teaching thinking. Teachers are empowered to make decisions that affect their jobs. Supervision, evaluation, and staff development practices enhance the perceptions and intellectual growth of certificated staff and honor their role as professional decision-makers (Costa and Garmston 1985; Costa, Garmston, and Lambert 1988).

Selection criteria for texts, tests, instructional materials, and other media include their contribution to thinking. Counseling, discipline, library, and psychological services are constantly evaluated for their enhancement of and consistency with thoughtful practice.

In schools and classrooms, discipline practices appeal to students' thoughtful behavior. Students participate in generating rational and compassionate classroom and school rules and continually strive to evaluate their own behavior in relation to those criteria (Curwin and Mendler 1988).

Protecting What's Important— Saying "No" to Distractions

Sometimes our vision of the desired school is temporarily blurred or obscured. We are distracted from our intellectual focus by fads, bandwagons, other educational "panaceas," and by pressures from public and vocal special-interest groups. Our purposes may be temporarily clouded by politically and financially expedient decisions. We must ignore all of these distractions as irrelevant to our central issue.

On the other hand, we need to encourage philosophical discussion because it gives voice to alternative views. Considering other perspectives—as expressed in such books as Bloom's *Closing of the American Mind* (1987), Ravitch and Finn's *What Do Our 17-Year-Olds Know?* (1987), and Hirsch's *Cultural Literacy* (1987)— creates tensions, honors divergent thinking, and expands and refines our vision. Such discussion encourages staff members to include modes of thinking and inquiring in their definition of literacy. Discussion strengthens the staff's commitment to the principle that to learn anything—to gain cultural literacy or basic skills—requires an engagement of the mind.

Knowing that thinking is the important goal, all inhabitants of the school believe that their right to think will be protected. District leaders keep this primary goal in focus as they make day-to-day decisions. Teachers' rights to be involved in the decisions affecting them are protected, as are the rights of those who choose not to be involved in decision making.

Since change and growth are viewed as intellectual processes, not events, we value the time invested in ownership, commitment, and learning.

Communications

Embedded in an organization's communications are expressions of what it prizes. Pick up any newspaper and you see a reflection of society's values in its major sections: sports, business and finance, and entertainment.

As a school becomes a home for the mind, the vision increasingly pervades all of its communications. In Palmdale, California and Pinellas Park, Florida report cards, parent conferences, and other progress reports include indicators of the growth of students' intelligent behaviors: questioning, metacognition, flexibility of thinking, persistence, listening to others' points of view, and creativity (Costa 1985b).

Growth in student's thinking abilities is assessed and reported in numerous ways, including teacher-made tests, structured observations, and interviews. Students maintain journals to record their own thinking and metacognition; they share, compare, and evaluate their own growth of insight, creativity, and problem-solving strategies over time. Parents, too, look for ways in which their children are transferring intellectual growth from the classroom to family and home situations. In Westover Elementary school in Stamford, Connecticut, portfolios of students' work show how their organizational abilities, conceptual develop-

ment, and creativity are growing. Test scores report such critical thinking skills as vocabulary growth, syllogistic thinking, reasoning by analogy, problem solving, and fluency.

Parents and community members in Sorento, Illinois, receive newspaper articles, calendars, and newsletters informing them of the school's intent and ways they can engage children's intellect (Diamandis and Obermark 1987-1988). "The Rational Enquirer" is the name given to the Auburn, Washington School District's Thinking Skills network newsletter. In Verona, Wisconsin, parents attend evening meetings to learn how to enhance their children's intelligent capacities and behaviors (Feldman 1986).

Mottoes, slogans, and mission statements are visible everywhere. "Lincoln Schools Are Thought-full Schools" is painted on one district's delivery trucks for all to see. In the Plymouth-Canton, Michigan, Public Schools, the superintendent distributes bookmarks reminding the community that thinking is the schools' goal; "Thought Taught At Huntington Beach High" is emblazoned on that school's note pads. "Making Thinking Happen" is printed on Calvin Coolidge Elementary School's letterhead in Shrewsbury, Massachusetts. "Thinking Spoken Here" is a constant classroom reminder of Stockton, California, history teacher Dan Theile's explicit goals for students. "We're Training Our Brains" is the motto on buttons proudly produced, sold, and worn by the special education students at Jamestown, Pennsylvania, Elementary School.

Tangible Support

How teachers, school administrators, and other leadership personnel expend their valuable and limited resources—time, energy, and money—signals the organization's value system. The Hanford, California, School Board provides a profound example of this point. The Board requires elementary school principals to spend 50 percent of their time in curriculum and activities related to instruction. To ensure that this happens administrative assistants were hired to provide support for principals.

The school that is becoming a home for the mind allocates financial resources to promote thinking. Irvine, California Schools hired a full-time thinking skills resource teacher. Substitutes are hired so that teachers can be released to visit and coach each other. Staff members and parents are sent to workshops, courses, conferences, and inservice sessions to learn more about effective thinking and the teaching of thinking.

Instructional materials and programs related to thinking are purchased, and time is provided to plan for and to train teachers in the use of these materials and to gather evidence of their effectiveness. Consultants discuss and report new learnings about intellectual development and implications for program improvement. Vignettes and "critical incidents" are recorded, described, and analyzed as indicators of students' application of critical and creative thinking skills and dispositions.

Administrators use their time and energy to visit classrooms to learn more about and to coach instruction in thinking. Teachers spend time planning lessons and observing each other teach for thinking. Time in classrooms, as well, is allocated to thinking skills and talking about thinking.

Thus, we see that the whole school community—students, teachers, administrators, classified personnel, board members, and parents—share a common vision of the school as a home for the mind. They continually work to sharpen that image, to clarify their goals, and to align daily practices with that vision of the future.

Process As Content

In the school that is becoming a home for the mind, development of the intellect, learning to learn, knowledge production, metacognition, decision making, creativity, and problem solving are the subject matter of instruction. Content is selected because of its contribution to process and thus becomes a vehicle for thinking processes.

*Problem Solving,
Decision Making,
and Open Communication*

Being committed to the improvement of intellectual growth, everyone in the school is willing to discuss their strategies for improving school climate, interpersonal relationships, and the quality of their interactions and problem solving. Students and school personnel practice, evaluate, and improve their listening skills of paraphrasing, empathizing, and clarifying and understanding.

At school board, administrative, and faculty meetings, decision-making processes are discussed, explained, and adopted. Process observers are invited to give feedback about the group's effectiveness and growth in decision-making, consensus-seeking, and communication skills.

Each group member's opinions and questions are respected. Disagreements are stated without fear of damaging relationships. Debates and critical assessment of alternate points of view are encouraged. Responsibility for "errors, omissions, and inadequacies" is accepted without blaming others. Responses are given and justified, and new ideas are advanced without fear of criticism or judgment. Group members' differing priorities, values, logic, and philosophical beliefs become the topics of analysis, dialogue, understanding, and further questions.

*Continuing to Learn—
Expanding the Knowledge Base*

Knowledge about thinking and the teaching of thinking is vast, complex, uncertain, and incomplete (Marzano, Brandt, Hughes, Jones, Presseisen, Rankin, and Suhor 1987). We will never know it all, nor would we wish to reduce teaching thinking to a simplistic, step-by-step lesson plan (Brandt 1987). In a school that is a home for the mind, the inhabitants continually expand their knowledge base: gaining more content, learning more about learning, and thinking more about thinking. They add to their repertoire of instructional skills and strategies, seeking greater diversity rather than conformity.

Knowing that the school's mission is to develop the intellect, teachers increasingly strive to invest thoughtful learning, craftsmanship, metacognition, and rigor into curriculum and instruction. They expand their repertoire of instructional skills and strategies to develop a wide range of reasoning, creative, and cooperative abilities in students.

Teachers increase their knowledge of the sciences, math, and humanities because it helps them ask more provocative questions that invite inquiry and critical thinking. A wider knowledge base supports the transfer of concepts across several subject areas and encourages appreciation for the disciplined methodologies of great thinkers throughout history.

8

Teachers draw from their growing repertoire of knowledge about instructional techniques and strategies to make decisions based on goals, students' characteristics, and the context in which they are working. They vary their lesson designs according to students' developmental levels, cognitive styles, and modality preferences (Jones 1987).

While their students expand their range of intelligent behaviors, teachers and administrators improve their own thinking skills and strategies by pursuing course work in philosophy, logic, and critical thinking. Thinking skills include not only knowing how to perform specific thought processes (Beyer 1985) but also knowing what to do when solutions to problems are not immediately known; study skills and learning-to-learn, reasoning, problem-solving, and decision-making strategies are important (Marzano and Arredondo 1986). Teachers and administrators learn about their own cognitive styles and how to cooperate with and value others who have differing styles. They learn how to cause their own "creative juices" to flow through brainstorming, inventing metaphor, synectics, and concept mapping.

Modeling

Thinking is probably best learned through imitation and emulation of good thinkers. Adults in the school that is becoming a home for the mind try to model the same qualities and behaviors they want students to develop. Teachers and administrators share their metacognitive strategies in the presence of students and others as they teach, plan, and solve problems (Jones 1987).

Staff members restrain their impulsiveness during emotional crises. They listen to students, parents, and each other with empathy, precision, and understanding. They reflect on and evaluate their own behaviors to make them more consistent with the core value that thoughtful behavior is a valid goal of education.

The School As A Community

Humans, as social beings, mature intellectually in reciprocal relationships with other people. Vygotsky (1978) points out that the higher functions actually originate in interactions with others.

> *Every function in...cultural development appears twice: first, on the social level, and later on the individual level; first between people (interpsychological), and then inside (intrapsychological). This applies equally to voluntary attention, to logical memory, and to the formation concepts. All the higher functions originate as actual relationships between individuals.*

Together, individuals generate and discuss ideas, eliciting thinking that surpasses individual effort. Together and privately, they express different perspectives, agree and disagree, point out and resolve discrepancies, and weigh alternatives. Because people grow by this process, collegiality is a crucial climate factor.

Collegiality

The essence of collegiality is that people in the school community are working together to better understand the nature of intelligent behavior. Professional collegiality at the district level is evident when administrators form support groups to assist each other; when teachers and administrators from different schools, subject areas, and grade levels form networks to coordinate efforts to enhance intelligent behavior across all content areas and in district policies and practices. Committees and advisory groups assess staff needs, identify and locate talent, and participate in district-level prioritizing and decision making. They support and provide liaison with school site efforts; plan district-wide inservice and articulation to enhance teachers' skills; and develop an aligned, coordinated, and developmentally appropriate curriculum for students.

Selection committees for instructional materials review and recommend adoption of materials and programs to enhance students' thinking. Through district-wide networks, teachers share information and materials and teach each other about skills, techniques, and strategies they have found to be effective. The staff at Tigard, Oregon, call this "Think Link."

In schools, teachers plan, prepare, and evaluate teaching materials. In St. Paul, Minnesota, teachers visit each other's classrooms frequently to coach and give feedback about the relationship between their instructional decisions and student behaviors. In Chugiak, Alaska, high school teachers are members of "instructional skills teams." Together they prepare, develop, remodel, and rehearse lessons. They then observe, coach, and give feedback to each other about their lessons.

Teachers and administrators continue to discuss and refine their vision of the school as a home for the mind. Definitions of thinking and the teaching and evaluation of students' intellectual progress are continually clarified. Child-study teams keep portfolios of students' work and discuss each student's developmental thought processes and learning styles. Teams explore instructional problems and generate experimental solutions. Faculty meetings are held in classrooms where the host teacher shares instructional practices, materials, and video-taped lessons with the rest of the faculty. Teacher teams sequence, articulate, and plan for continuity, reinforcement, and assessment of thinking skills across grade levels and subject areas.

An Environment of Trust

People are more likely to engage and grow in higher-level, creative, and experimental thought when they are in a trusting, risk-taking climate (Kohn 1987). MacLean's (1978) concept of the triune brain illuminates the need for operating in an environment of trust. For the neo-mammalian brain (the neo-cortex) to become fully engaged in its functions of problem solving, hypothesis formation, experimentation, and creativity, the reptilian brain (R-Complex) and the paleomammalian brain (limbic system) need to be in harmony. Under stress or trauma, the more basic survival needs demanded by the reptilian brain and the emotional security and personal identity required by the paleomammalian brain can override and disrupt the more complex neo-cortical functioning.

Because higher-order thinking is valued as a goal for everyone in the school, the school's climate is monitored continually for signs of stress that might close down complex and creative thinking. Risk-taking requires a nonjudgmental atmosphere where information can be shared without fear that it will be used to evaluate success or failure.

A climate of trust is evident when experiments are conducted with lesson designs, instructional sequences, and teaching materials to determine their effects on small groups of students (or with colleagues before they're used with a group). Various published programs and curriculums are pilot-tested, and evidence is gathered over time of the effects on students' growth in thinking skills. Teachers become researchers when alternate classroom arrangements and instructional strategies are tested and colleagues observe student interactions.

Appreciation and Recognition

Whether a work of art, athletic prowess, an act of heroism, or a precious jewel, what is valued in society is given public recognition. Core values are communicated when people see what is appreciated. If thinking is valued, it, too, is recognized by appreciation expressed to students and to teachers and administrators as well.

Students are recognized for persevering, striving for precision and accuracy, cooperating, considering another person's point of view, planning ahead, and expressing empathy. Students applaud each other for acts of ingenuity, compassion, and persistence. The products of their creativity, cooperation, and thoughtful investigation are displayed throughout the school.

Teachers at Wasatch Elementary School in Salt Lake City award blue ribbons to students who display intelligent behaviors. Similarly, teachers in East Orange, New Jersey, give certificates for "good thinking."

11

One form of appreciation is to invite teachers to describe their successes and unique ways of organizing for teaching thinking. In faculty meetings, teachers share videotaped lessons and showcase the positive results of their lesson planning, strategic teaching, and experimentation.

Schools within the district receive banners, flags, trophies, or certificates of excellence for their persistence, thoughtful actions, creativity, cooperative efforts, or meritorious service to the community. Some schools have even established a "Thinkers Hall of Fame."

Sharing, Caring, and Celebrating
Thinking skills are pervasive in schools that value thinking. They are visible in the traditions, celebrations, and everyday events of school life.

Staff members are often overheard sharing humorous anecdotes of students who display their thought processes. ("I saw two 7th grade boys on the athletic field yesterday ready to start duking it out. Before I could get to them, another boy intervened and said, 'Hey, you guys, restrain your impulsivity.'")

Teachers and administrators share personal, humorous, and sometimes embarrassing anecdotes of their own problems with thinking (tactics for remembering peoples' names, finding their car in the parking lot, or solving the dilemma of locking the keys in the car.)

At career days, local business and industry leaders describe what reasoning, creative problem solving, and cooperative skills are needed in various jobs. At school assemblies, students and teachers are honored for acts of creativity, cooperation, thoughtfulness, innovation, and scholarly accomplishments. Academic decathlons, thinking and science fairs, problem-solving tournaments, dialogical debates, invention conventions, art exhibits, and musical programs all celebrate the benefits of strategic planning, careful research, insightfulness, sustained practice, and cooperative efforts.

The Ultimate Purpose: Enhancing Student Thinking

A common vision, process as content, and the school as a community are not ends in themselves. We must constantly remind ourselves that the reason we construct our schools is to serve our youth.

As cornerstones and building blocks of school climate are gradually cemented into a sturdy foundation, teachers will in turn create a classroom with corresponding climate factors that recognize and support growth in students' intelligent behaviors.

The vision of education as the development of critical thinking abilities is evident as students deliberate and persevere in their problem solving, as they work to make their oral and written work more precise and accurate, as they consider others' points of view, as they generate questions, and as they explore the alternatives and consequences of their actions. Students engage in increasingly rigorous learning activities that challenge the intellect and imagination. Such scholarly pursuits require the acquisition, comprehension, and application of new knowledge and activate the need for perseverance, research, and increasingly complex forms of problem solving.

Since such processes of thinking as problem solving, strategic reasoning, and decision making are explicitly stated as the content of lessons, they become the "tasks that students are on." The metacognitive processes engaged in while learning and applying the knowledge are discussed. Thus students' thinking becomes more conscious, more reflective, more efficient, more flexible, and more transferable.

Collegiality is evident as students work together cooperatively with their "study-buddies," in learning groups, and in peer problem solving. In class meetings, students are observed learning to set goals, establish plans, and set priorities. They generate, hold, and apply criteria for assessing the growth of their own thoughtful behavior. They take risks, experiment

with ideas, share thinking strategies (metacognition), and venture forth with creative thoughts without fear of being judged. Value judgments and criticisms are replaced by accepting, listening, empathizing with, and clarifying each other's ideas (Costa 1985a).

The Greeks had a word for it: *paideia*. The term, popularized by Adler's *Proposal* (1983), is an ideal concept we share: a school in which learning, fulfillment, and becoming more humane are the primary goals for all students, faculty, and support staff. It is the Athenian concept of a learning society in which self-development, intellectual empowerment, and lifelong learning are esteemed core values and all institutions within the culture are constructed to contribute to those goals.

References

Adler, M. J. *The Paideia Proposal: An Educational Manifesto.* New York, NY: Macmillan, 1983.

Beyer, B. "Teaching Critical Thinking: A Direct Approach." *Social Education,* 49(4), 297-303, April 1985.

Bloom, A. *The Closing of the American Mind.* New York, NY: Simon and Schuster, 1987.

Boyer, E. "On the High School Curriculum: A Conversation with Ernest Boyer." *Educational Leadership*, 46(1), September 1988.

Brandt, R. "On Teaching Thinking Skills: A Conversation with B. Othanel Smith." *Educational Leadership*, 45, October 1987.

Costa, A. "Teacher Behaviors That Enhance Thinking." In A. Costa (Ed.), *Developing Minds: A Resource Book for Teaching Thinking*. Alexandria, VA: Association for Supervision and Curriculum Development, 1985a.

Costa, A. "How Can We Recognize Improved Student Thinking?" In A. Costa (Ed.), *Developing Minds: A Resource Book for Teaching Thinking*. Alexandria, VA: Association for Supervision and Curriculum Development, 1985b.

Costa, A. and Garmston, R. "Supervision for Intelligent Teaching." *Educational Leadership*, 42(5), 70-80, February 1985.

Costa, A.; Garmston, R.; and Lambert, L. "Teacher Evaluation: A Cognitive Development View." In S. Stanley and J. Popham (Eds.), *Teacher Evaluation: Six Prescriptions for Success*. Alexandria, VA: Association for Supervision and Curriculum Development, 1988.

Curwin, R. and Mendler, A. *Discipline with Dignity*. Alexandria, VA: Association for Supervision and Curriculum Development, 1989.

Deal, T. Presentation made at the 1987 ASCD Annual Conference, New Orleans, LA, 1987.

Diamandis, L. and Obermark, C. "Bright Ideas—A Newsletter for Parents: Critical Thinking Activities for Kindergarten Children." Sorento, IL, II(2), December-January 1987-1988.

Feldman, R. D. "How to Improve Your Child's Intelligent Behavior." *Woman's Day*, 62-68, November 11, 1986.

Goodlad, J. I. *A Place Called School: Prospects for the Future*. New York, NY: McGraw Hill, 1984.

Harmon, W. *Global Mind Change*. Indianapolis, IN: Knowledge Systems, Inc. Published in cooperation with the Institute of Noetic Sciences, Sausalito, CA, 1988.

Hirsch, E. D. *Cultural Literacy*. Boston, MA: Houghton Mifflin, 1987.

Jones, B. F. "Strategic Teaching: A Cognitive Focus." In B. F. Jones, A. S. Palincsar, D. Ogle, and E. Carr (Eds.), *Strategic Teaching and Learning: Cognitive Instruction in the Content Areas*. Alexandria, VA: Association for Supervision and Curriculum Development, 1987.

Kohn, A. "Art for Art's Sake." *Psychology Today*, 21, 52-57, September 1987.

MacLean, P. "A Mind of Three Minds: Educating the Triune Brain." In J. Chall and A. Mirsky (Eds.), *Education and the Brain.* Chicago, IL: University of Chicago Press, 1987.

Marzano, R. and Arredondo, D. *Tactics for Thinking.* Alexandria, VA: Association for Supervision and Curriculum Development, 1986.

Marzano, R.; Brands, R.; Hughes, C.; Jones, B. F.; Presseisen, B.; Rankin, S.; and Suhor, C. *Dimensions of Thinking.* Alexandria, VA: Association for Supervision and Curriculum Development, 1987.

McClure, R. *Visions of School Renewal.* Washington, DC: National Education Association, 1988.

Pascarella, P. *The New Achievers.* New York, NY: Free Press, 1984.

Perkins, D. *The Mind's Best Work: A New Psychology of Creative Thinking.* Cambridge, MA: Harvard University Press, 1983.

Ravitch, D. and Finn, C. *What Do Our 17-Year-Olds Know?* New York, NY: Harper and Row, 1987.

Saphier, J. "Strengthening School Culture." Presentation made at the 1987 ASCD Annual Conference, New Orleans, LA, 1987.

Saphier, J. and King, M. "Good Seeds Grow in Strong Cultures." *Educational Leadership.* Vol. 42(6), 67-74, March 1985.

Sizer, T. *Horace's Compromise: The Dilemma of the American High School.* Boston, MA: Houghton Mifflin, 1984.

Vygotsky, L. *Society of Mind.* Cambridge, MA: Harvard University Press, 1978.

———— ✿ ————

Aesthetics: Where Thinking Originates

All information gets to the brain through our sensory channels—our tactile, gustatory, olfactory, visual, kinesthetic, and auditory senses. Those whose sensory pathways are open, alert, and acute absorb more information from the environment than those whose pathways are withered, immune, and oblivious to sensory stimuli. It is proposed, therefore, that *aesthetics* is an essential element of thinking skills programs. Cognitive education should include the development of sensory acumen.

Permeating the spirit of inquiry, inherent in creativity, and prerequisite to discovery, the aesthetic dimensions of thought have received little concern or attention as a part of cognitive instruction. The addition of aesthetics implies that learners become not only cognitively involved, but also enraptured with the phenomena, principles, and discrepancies they encounter in their environment. In order for the brain to comprehend, the heart must first listen.

Aesthetics, as used here, means sensitivity to the artistic features of the environment and the qualities of experience that evoke feelings in individuals. Such feelings include enjoyment, exhilaration, awe, and satisfaction. Thus, aesthetics is the sensitive beginning of rational thought, which leads to enlightenment about the complexities of our environment. It may be that from within the aesthetic realm the skills of observing, investigating, and questioning germinate. These are bases for further scientific inquiry. Aesthetics may be the key to sustaining motivation, interest, and enthusiasm in young children; since they must become aware of their environment before they can explain it, use it wisely, and adjust to it. With the addition of aesthetics, cognition shifts from a mere passive comprehension to a tenacious quest.

Children need many opportunities to commune with the world around them. Time needs to be allotted for children to reflect on the changing formations of a cloud, to be charmed by the opening of a bud, and to sense the logical simplicity of mathematical order. They must find beauty in a sunset, intrigue in the geometrics of a spider web, and exhilaration in the iridescence of a hummingbird's wings. They must see the congruity and intricacies in the derivation of a mathematical formula, recognize the orderliness and adroitness of a chemical change, and commune with the serenity of a distant constellation.

We need to observe and nurture these aesthetic qualities in children. Students who respond to the aesthetic aspects of their world will demonstrate behaviors manifesting such intangible values. They will derive more pleasure from thinking as they advance to higher grade levels. Their curiosity will become stronger as the problems they encounter become more complex. Their environment will attract their inquiry as their senses capture the rhythm, patterns, shapes, colors, and harmonies of the universe. They will display cognizant and compassionate behavior toward other life forms as they are able to understand the need for protecting their environment; respecting the roles and values of other human beings; and perceiving the delicate worth, uniqueness, and relationships of everything and everyone they encounter. After the period of inspiration comes the phase of execution; as children explore, investigate, and observe, their natural curiosity

leads them to ask "What?" "How?" "Why?" and "What if?"

Children need help in developing this feeling for, awareness of, and intuitiveness about the forces affecting the universe—the vastness of space, the magnitude of time, and the dynamics of change. But can this attitude be taught in specific lesson plans and instructional models? Are steps for its development written in method books? Can we construct instructional theory for cognitive education that includes aesthetics as a basis for learning? Or do children derive this attitude from their associations and interactions with significant other adults who exhibit it?

Perhaps we need to identify teachers who approach thinking with an aesthetic sense. It may be teachers who generate awareness of the outside world in children. They are often the underlying inspiration for children to become ardent observers and insatiable questioners. Teachers may be the ones who develop in others a compassionate attitude toward the environment and a curiosity with which they go wondering through life—a prerequisite for higher-level thought.

The Search For Intelligent Life

Time and energy devoted to clarifying definitions of thinking skills and abilities are well spent. If we know what our outcomes are, we can more readily select or construct learning experiences that contribute to them and determine what student behaviors indicate that those goals are being achieved. I suggest that the goals of cognitive education should be the achievement of those dispositions, attitudes, or inclinations that are characteristic of intelligently behaving human beings.

Some Assumptions About Intelligent Behaviors

In teaching for thinking, we are interested not only in what students know but also in how students behave when they don't know. Intelligent behavior is demonstrated when we are confronted with questions and problems for which we don't know the immediate answer. We want students to use what they learn to solve all kinds of problems—new and old.

By definition, a problem is any stimulus, question, task, phenomenon, anomaly, discrepancy, or perplexing situation. We want to focus on student performance under challenging conditions that demand strategic reasoning, insightfulness, perseverance, creativity, and craftsmanship to resolve complex problems.

Gathering evidence of the performance and growth of intelligent behavior is difficult through standardized testing. It really requires "kid-watching": observing students as they try to solve the day-to-day academic and real-life problems they encounter in school, at home, on the playground, alone, and with friends. By collecting anecdotes and examples of written, oral, and visual expressions, we can see students' increasingly voluntary and spontaneous performance of these intelligent behaviors.

The Search for Intelligent Behaviors

Just what do human beings do when they behave intelligently? In their research in effective thinking and intelligent behavior, Feuerstein, Rand, Hoffman, and Miller (1980), Glatthorn and Baron (1985), Sternberg (1984), Perkins (1985), and Ennis (1985) found that effective thinkers share identifiable characteristics. These characteristics have been identified in successful mechanics, teachers, entrepreneurs, salespeople, parents—people from all walks of life.

Below are 14 characteristics of intelligent behavior that teachers and parents can teach and observe. This list is not meant to be complete, but rather suggestive of the goals for which we are striving. As we think and study more about intelligent behavior we will undoubtedly discover additional characteristics.

1. Persistence

Failed in business	*1831*
defeated for legislature	*1832*
again failed in business	*1833*
elected to legislature	*1834*
defeated for Speaker	*1838*
defeated for elector	*1840*
defeated for Congress	*1843*
elected to Congress	*1846*
defeated for Congress	*1848*
defeated for Senate	*1855*
defeated for vice-president	*1858*
defeated for Senate	*1858*
elected president of the United States in 1860—Abraham Lincoln	

People who behave intelligently try to stick to a task until it is completed. They don't give up easily. For instance, when asked how he was able to discover the law of universal gravitation, Sir Isaac Newton disarmingly replied, "By thinking on it continuously." Some students, however, when they can't immediately find the answer to a problem, crumple their papers and throw them away, saying, "I can't do this, it's too hard," or they make up an answer to get the task over with as quickly as possible. They lack the ability to analyze a problem, to develop a system, structure, or strategy of problem attack. I overhead one student, when challenged with a provocative problem, say, "I don't do thinking!"

Students demonstrate growth in thinking abilities by increasing their use of alternative strategies of problem solving. They collect evidence to indicate their problem-solving strategy is working, and if one strategy doesn't work, they know how to back up and try another. They realize that they must reject their theory or idea and employ another. They have systematic methods of analyzing a problem, knowing ways to begin, knowing what steps must be performed, and what data need to be generated or collected. This is what is meant by perseverance.

2. Decreasing Impulsivity

By the time I think about what I'm going to do, I already did it.
—Dennis the Menace

When it is important to do so, intelligent people think before they act. They deliberately form a vision of a product, a plan of action, a goal, or a destination before they begin.

In school, however, students often blurt out the first answer that comes to mind. Sometimes they shout an answer, start to work without fully understanding directions, work without an organized plan or strategy for approaching a problem, or make immediate value judgments about an idea—criticizing or praising it—before fully understanding it. They take the first suggestion given or operate on the first idea that comes to mind rather than consider alternatives and consequences of several possible solutions.

As students become less impulsive, we can observe them clarifying goals, planning a strategy for solving a problem, exploring alternative problem-solving strategies, and considering the consequences of action before they begin. They use fewer trial-and-error tactics, gather information before they begin a task, take time to reflect on an answer before giving it, make sure they understand directions before starting a task, and listen to alternative points of view.

3. Listening to Others—With Understanding and Empathy

The way of being with another person which is termed empathic means temporarily living in their life, moving about in it delicately, without making judgments. To be with another person in this way means that for the time being you lay aside the views and values you hold for yourself in order to enter the other's world without prejudice. A complex, demanding, strong yet subtle and gentle way of being.
—Carl Rogers

Some psychologists believe that the ability to listen to other people, to empathize with and to understand their point of view, is one of the highest forms of intelligent behavior. Being able to paraphrase other people's ideas; detecting indicators (cues) of their feelings or emotional states in their oral and body language (empathy); accurately expressing other people's concepts, emotions, and problems—all are indications of listening behaviors (Piaget called it "overcoming ego-centrism").

Some students ridicule other students' ideas. They are unable to build on, consider the merits of, or operate on another person's ideas. We know students are developing better listening skills when we observe them attending to another person and demonstrating an understanding of, or empathy for, another person's idea or feeling by accurately paraphrasing it, building on it, clarifying it, or giving an example of it. When students say, "Peter's idea is…, but Sarah's idea is…," or "Let's try Shelley's idea and see if it works," or "Let me show you how Gina solved the problem, then I'll show you how I solved it," then we know students are listening to and internalizing others' ideas and feelings.

4. Cooperative Thinking— Social Intelligence

> *Getting along well with other people is still the world's most needed skill. With it . . . there is no limit to what a person can do. We need people, we need the cooperation of others. There is very little we can do alone.*
> —Earl Nightingale

Humans are social beings. We congregate in groups, find it therapeutic to be listened to, draw energy from one another, and seek reciprocity. In groups, we contribute our time and energy to tasks that we would quickly tire of when working alone. In fact, one of the cruelest forms of punishment we can inflict is solitary confinement.

Humans who behave intelligently realize that all of us together are more powerful than any one of us. Probably the foremost of intelligent behaviors for the post-industrial society will be a heightened ability to think in concert with others. As the world population steadily grows and we find ourselves living together in increasingly closer proximity, we will become ever more conscious that the earth is a closed ecological system and that sensitivity to the needs of others is paramount to human survival.

Problem solving has become so complex that no one person can go it alone. No one has access to all the data needed to make critical decisions; no one person can consider as many alternatives as several people. But working in groups requires the ability to justify ideas and to test the feasibility of solution strategies on others. Indeed, there are not many decisions any of us makes without having to consider their effects on others.

Children do not necessarily come to school knowing how to work effectively in groups. They may exhibit competitiveness, narrow-mindedness, egocentrism, ethnocentrism, or criticism of others' values, emotions, and beliefs.

Listening, consensus seeking, giving up an idea to work on someone else's, empathy, compassion, group leadership, knowing how to support group efforts, altruism—all are behaviors indicative of intelligent human beings.

5. Flexibility in Thinking

> *To raise new questions, new problems, to regard old problems from a new angle requires creative imagination and makes real advances.*
> —Albert Einstein

Intelligent people can approach a problem from a new angle using a novel approach. De Bono (1970) refers to this as *lateral thinking.*

Some students have difficulty in considering alternative points of view or dealing with several sources of information simultaneously. Their way to solve a problem seems to be the only way. They may decide that their answer is the only correct answer. They are most interested in knowing the correctness of their answer than in being challenged by the process of finding the answer. They are unable to sustain a process of problem solving over time, so they avoid ambiguous situations; they have a need for certainty rather than an inclination to doubt. Their minds are made up and they resist being influenced by data or reasoning that contradicts their beliefs.

As students become more flexible in their thinking they can be heard considering, expressing, or paraphrasing another person's point of view or rationale. They can state several ways of solving the same problem and can evaluate the merits and consequences of alternative courses of action. When making decisions, they will often use such words as "however," "on the other hand," or "if you look at it another way." Although they gradually develop a set of moral principles to govern their own behavior, they are willing to change their mind if presented with a convincing argument. Working in groups, they often resolve conflicts through compromise, express a willingness to experiment with another person's idea, and strive for consensus.

6. Metacognition—Awareness of One's Own Thinking

When the mind is thinking it is talking to itself.
—Plato

Some people are unaware of their own thinking processes while they are thinking. When asked, "How are you solving that problem?" they may reply, "I don't know, I'm just doing it." They can't describe the steps and sequences that they use before, during, or after problem solving. They can't transform into words the visual images held in their mind. They seldom plan for, reflect on, and evaluate the quality of their own thinking skills and strategies.

By asking students to describe what goes on in their head while they are thinking, we determine if students are becoming more aware of their thinking. When asked, they should be able to:

- describe what they know and what they need to know

- describe what data are lacking and their plans for producing those data

- describe their plan of action before they begin to solve a problem

- list the steps and tell where they are in the sequence of a problem strategy

- trace the pathways and blind alleys they took on the road to problem solution

They should also learn to apply cognitive vocabulary correctly as they describe their thinking skills and strategies using such phrases as:

- "I have a hypothesis…"

- "My theory is…"

- "When I compare these points of view…"

- "By way of summary…"

- "What I need to know is…"

- "The assumptions on what I am working are…"

7. Striving for Accuracy and Precision

A man who has committed a mistake and doesn't correct it is committing another mistake.
—Confucius

Intelligent people want to communicate accurately in both written and oral form. Often, however, we use language that is vague and imprecise, describing objects or events with words like *weird, nice,* or *OK,* calling specific objects *stuff,* *junk,* and *things,* and punctuating sentences with meaningless interjections like *ya know, er,* and *uh.*

We use vague or general nouns and pronouns ("*They* told me to." "*Everybody* has one." "*Teachers* don't understand me."), nonspecific verbs ("Let's *do* it."), and unqualified comparatives ("This soda is *better,* I like it *more.*").

Unless prompted, students rarely review their papers before turning them in. They seem to feel little inclination to reflect upon the accuracy of their work, to take pride in their accomplishments. Their desire to get the assignment over with surpasses their pleasure in craftsmanship.

We can observe students growing in their desire for accuracy:

- They take time to check over their tests and papers.

- They review the rules by which they are to abide.

- They review the models and visions they are to follow.

- They review the criteria they are to employ, and they confirm that their finished product matches the criteria exactly.

As students' language becomes more precise, we hear them using more descriptive words to distinguish attributes. They use correct names and when universal labels are unavailable, they use relevant analogies. They spontaneously provide criteria for their own value judgments and describe why they think one product is better than another. They speak in complete sentences, voluntarily provide supporting evidence for their ideas, and elaborate, clarify, and operationally define their terminology. Their oral and written expression become more concise, descriptive, and coherent.

8. A Sense of Humor

I bought my grandson some war toys; you know, rocket launchers, laser guns, star-wars stuff. Gee, they were realistic: expensive, complicated, and they didn't work.

—Anonymous

Laughter transcends all human beings. Its positive effects on physiological functions include a drop in the pulse rate, the secretion of endorphins, and increased oxygen in the blood. It has been found to liberate creativity and provide such high-level thinking skills as anticipation, finding novel relationships, and visual imagery.

The acquisition of a sense of humor follows a developmental sequence similar to that described by Piaget (1972) and Kohlberg (1981). We may observe some students whose sense of humor has not yet been fully developed. They laugh at all the wrong things—human frailty, ethnic humor, sacrilegious riddles, and ribald profanities.

People who behave intelligently have the ability to perceive situations from an original and often humorous vantage point. They tend to initiate humor more often, to place greater value on having a sense of humor, to appreciate and understand others' humor, and to be verbally playful when interacting with others. They thrive on finding incongruity and have a whimsical frame of mind that is characteristic of creative problem solvers (Cornett 1986).

9. Questioning and Problem Posing

The formulation of a problem is often more essential than its solution, which may be merely a matter of mathematical or experimental skills.
—Albert Einstein

Someone asked the Nobel Laureate I. I. Rabi why he became a physicist, rather than a doctor or a lawyer or a tailor, like his father. Rabi explained that his mother made him a scientist without ever intending it. Every other Jewish mother in Brooklyn would ask her child, "So? What did you learn in school today?" But not his mother. She always asked, "Izzi, what good questions did you ask today?" (Barell 1988).

One of the characteristics that distinguishes humans from other forms of life is our inclination and our ability to *find* problems to solve. Yet students often depend on others to solve problems, to find answers, and to ask questions for them. They sometimes are reluctant to ask questions for fear of displaying ignorance.

Over time, we want to observe a shift from the teacher's asking questions and posing problems toward the students' asking questions and finding problems for themselves. Furthermore, the types of questions students ask should change and become more specific and profound. For example, students should ask for data to support others' conclusions and assumptions—using such questions as "What evidence do you have?" or "How do you know that's true?" And they should pose more hypothetical problems characterized by "if" questions: "What do you think would happen if...?" or "If that is true, then what might happen if...?"

We want students to be alert to, and recognize, discrepancies and phenomena in their environment and to inquire about their causes: "Why do cats purr?" "How high can birds fly?" "Why does the hair on my head grow fast, while the hair on my arms and legs grows slowly?" "What would happen if we put the saltwater fish in a freshwater aquarium?" "Besides war, what are some possible solutions to international conflicts?"

10. Drawing on Past Knowledge and Applying It to New Situations

If the processes don't transfer, they cannot be even be called THINKING. They can be called LEARNING, MEMORY, or HABIT, but not thinking. The purpose of a course on thinking is to enhance students' abilities to face new challenges and to attach novel problems confidently, rationally, and productively.
—Marilyn J. Adams (1989)

The ultimate goal of teaching is for students to apply school-learned knowledge to real-life situations and to content areas beyond those in which it was learned. Yet we find that even though students can, for example, pass the mastery tests in mathematics, they often have difficulty deciding whether to buy six items for $2.39 or seven for $2.86 at the supermarket.

Too often students begin a task as if they were approaching it for the very first time. Teachers are often dismayed when they invite students to recall how they solved a similar problem and students don't remember, even though they've recently solve the same type of problem. They act as though they've never head of it before. It's as if each experience is encapsulated into a separate episode that has no relationship to anything that came before or that comes afterward.

Intelligent human beings learn from experience. They abstract meaning from their experiences and apply it in new situations. When students say, "This reminds me of..." or "This is just like the time when I...," they show that they are developing this ability. They explain what they are doing by using analogies and references to previous experiences. They call on their store of knowledge and experience as sources of data to support, theories to explain, or processes to solve each new challenge.

When parents and other teachers report how they have observed students thinking at home or in other classes, we know students are transferring. For example: parents report their child's increased interest in school, better use of time and finances, and improved organization of books and other belongings at home. (One parent reported that during a slumber party, his daughter invited her friends to "brainstorm" which activities and games they preferred. This happened after she learned brainstorming techniques in school.)

We might hear, for example, the social studies teacher describe how a student used a problem-solving strategy that was originally learned in the science class. We might hear the woodshop teacher tell how a student volunteered a plan to measure accurately before cutting a piece of wood: "Measure twice and cut once," an axiom learned in algebra class.

11. Risk Taking

We can never discover new continents until we have the courage to lose sight of all coasts.
—André Gide

Intelligent people seem to have an almost uncontrollable urge to go beyond established limits. Dick Fosbury was such a person. In the early 1960s, this young, lanky Oregon athlete wouldn't high-jump like everyone else. Fosbury insisted on going over the bar backwards and head first. His unorthodox technique, which came to be know as the "Fosbury Flop," not only won him an Olympic gold medal, it also became the standard practice for future athletes, who broke records with jumps that experts believed were unattainable.

David Perkins (1985) states that creative people are uneasy with the status quo; they "live on the edge of their competence." They seem compelled to place themselves in situations where they don't know what is going to happen. They accept confusion, uncertainty, and the higher risks of failure, as part of the process and learn to view failure as normal, even interesting and challenging.

Students often display a reluctance to venture forth with ideas or statements that might be considered bizarre or far-out. They feel more comfortable knowing that they are "correct" and often demand to know whether their

27

answers are "right," rather enjoy the feeling of sustained uncertainty. They hesitate to respond to open-ended questions, fearing that they will not give the "correct" answers. Students often report feeling more secure when they can apply already known rules or algorithms, rather than when they have to compose their own.

Students demonstrate their risk-taking ability as they gain security in brainstorming, offering novel relation-ships, sharing original thoughts, tackling new problems, and requesting *not* to be given an answer because they want to figure it out for themselves.

12. Using All the Senses

> *Observe perpetually.*
> —Henry James

Language, culture, and physical learning are all derived from our senses. To know a wine it must be drunk; to know a role it must be acted; to know a game it must be played; to know a dance it must be moved; to know a goal it must be envisioned. Those whose sensory pathways are open and alert absorb more informa-tion from the environment than those whose pathways are oblivious to sensory stimuli.

We can observe students using their senses when they touch objects in their environment, when they request that a story or rhyme be read again and again,

or when they act out roles. Often, what they say tells us that their senses are engaged: "Let me see, let me see…" "I want to feel it…" "Let me try it…" "Let me hold it…"

As children mature, we can observe that they conceive and express many ways of solving problems by the use of the senses: Making observations, gathering data, experimenting, manipulating, scrutinizing, identifying variables, interviewing, breaking problems down into components, visualizing, role playing, illustrating, or model building. Their expressions use a range and variety of sensory words: "I *feel* like…" "It *touches* me," "I *hear* your ideas," "It leaves a bad *taste* in my mouth," "Get the *picture?*"

13. Ingenuity, Originality, Insightfulness: Creativity

> *It is by logic that we prove, but by intuition that we discover.*
> —Leo Rosten

Intelligent human beings know how to be creative when the situation demands it. They often try to create different solutions to problems, examining alternative possibilities from many angles (lateral thinking). They tend to project themselves into differ-ent roles, starting with a vision and working backward to their "solution."

We often hear students (and adults), however, saying things like "I can't draw," "I was never very good at art," or "I can't sing a note." Many people believe that creativity lies in a person's genes and chromosomes, but we are coming to realize that all of us have the capacity to generate novel, original, clever or ingenious products, solutions, and techniques—if that capacity is consciously developed.

Intelligent people are intrinsically rather than extrinsically motivated. Fame and glory don't seem to drive most creative people. Rather, it is the rewards of the work—the fascination of mixing paint or combining sounds or manipulating numbers. They work on the task because of its aesthetic challenges rather than its material rewards.

Creative people are open to criticism. They hold up their products for others to judge and seek feedback in an ever increasing effort to refine their technique (Perkins 1985). They constantly strive for greater fluency, elaboration, novelty, parsimony, simplicity, craftsmanship, perfection, beauty, harmony, or balance.

14. Wonderment, Inquisitiveness, Curiosity, and the Enjoyment of Problem Solving—A Sense of Efficacy as a Thinker

All thinking begins with wonderment.
—Socrates

People performing at their peak seem to enter another world.

Time becomes distorted and a sense of euphoria prevails. They report a sense of feeling alive and fully alert. Athletes talk of a "runner's high" or "entering the zone." Creative people often experience similar periods of euphoria in their work, and it may be that their unconscious internal motivation is the desire to recapture this euphoria.

Many people don't let themselves feel wonder and curiosity in the face of problems, and thus, they don't enjoy the challenge of solving problems. They may say, "These types of thinking games turn me off," "I was never good at these brainteasers," or "Go ask your father, he's the brain in this family." In high school or college, these people never enrolled in math or other "hard" academic subjects if they didn't have to. They perceive thinking only as hard work and recoil from situations that demand "too much" of it.

We want students to move toward not only an "I *can*" attitude, but also toward an "I *enjoy*" feeling. We want them to seek problems to solve for themselves and to give to others to solve; to make up problems to solve on their own and to request them from others. Furthermore, we want students to solve problems with increasing interdependence—without parents' or teachers' help or intervention. We want them to voluntarily continue to learn throughout a lifetime, for if they don't, then the school has failed them.

Children (and adults) must actively sense the world around them, not just let it pass by. The wonders of nature promote endless thought—the changing of the seasons, the life cycle of a butterfly, the physics behind a bird in flight, the passing of day into night.

As students advance to higher grade levels, they should derive even more pleasure from thinking. Their curiosity will become stronger as the problems they encounter become more complex. Their environment will attract their inquiry as their senses capture the rhythm, patterns, shapes, colors, and harmonies of the universe. They will display cognizant and compassionate behavior toward other life forms as they are able to understand the need for protecting their environment, respecting the roles and values of other human beings, and perceiving the delicate worth, uniqueness, and relationships of everything and everyone they encounter. Passion, wonderment, a sense of awe: these are the prerequisites for intelligent life.

References

Adams, M.J. "Thinking Skills Curricula: Their Promise and Progress." *Educational Psychologist* 24, 1: 25-77. Hillsdale, NJ: Erlbaum, 1989.

Barell, J. *Cogitare: A Newsletter of the ASCD Network on Teaching Thinking* 3, 1: entire issue, April, 1988.

Cornett, C. *Learning Through Laughter: Humor in the Classroom.* Bloomington, IA: Phi Delta Kappa Educational Foundation, 1986.

de Bono, E. *Lateral Thinking: Creativity Step by Step.* New York: Harper and Row, 1970.

Ennis, R. "Goals for a Critical Thinking Curriculum" *Developing Minds: A Resource Book for Teaching Thinking,* edited by A.L. Costa. Alexandria, VA: Association for Supervision and Curriculum Development, 1985.

Feuerstein, R.; Rand, Y.; Hoffman, M.; and Miller, R. "Instrumental Enrichment" *An Intervention Program for Cognitive Modifiability.* Baltimore, MD.: University Park Press, 1980.

Glatthorn, A. and Baron, J. "The Good Thinker." *Developing Minds: A Resource Book for Teaching Thinking,* edited by A.L. Costa, Alexandria, VA: Association for Supervision and Curriculum Development, 1985.

Kohlberg, I. *The Meaning and Measurement of Moral Development.* Worcester, MA: Clark University Press, 1981.

Perkins, D. "What Creative Thinking Is." *Developing Minds: A Resource Book for Teaching Thinking,* edited by A.L. Costa, Alexandria, VA: Association for

Supervision and Curriculum Development, 1985.

Piaget, J. *The Psychology of Intelligence.* Totowa, NJ: Littlefield Adams, 1972.

Sternberg, R. *Beyond IQ: A Triarchic Theory of Human Intelligence.* New York: Cambridge University Press, 1984.

———— 🙠 ————

Section II

The Thoughtful Curriculum

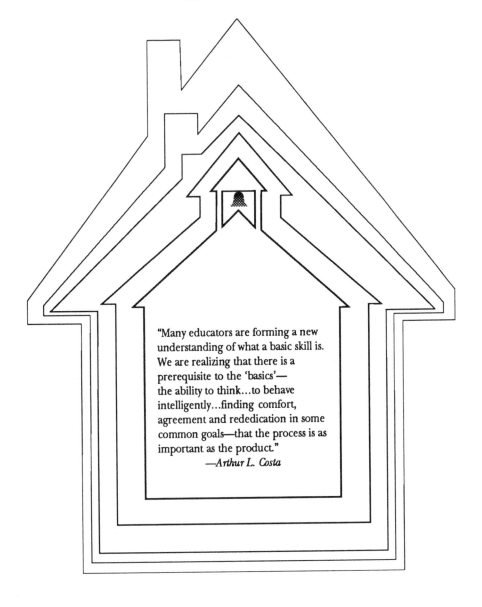

"Many educators are forming a new
understanding of what a basic skill is.
We are realizing that there is a
prerequisite to the 'basics'—
the ability to think...to behave
intelligently...finding comfort,
agreement and rededication in some
common goals—that the process is as
important as the product."
—*Arthur L. Costa*

4

Teaching For, Of, And About Thinking

Ron Brandt's editorial in the September 1984 issue of *Educational Leadership* is one of the most helpful organizers for the teaching of thinking I've found. He discusses a balanced, three-part program, which I interpret as follows.

Teaching FOR Thinking

Many authors and psychologists feel that children learn to think long before they come to school and that educators need to create the conditions for their natural, human inclination to think to emerge and develop. Indeed, Hart (1975) believes that schools are "brain incompatible." In their studies of creativity, Ghiselin and Gardner find that what young children do prior to entering school and what practicing scientists and artists do is more similar than anything that goes on in between.

Teaching for thinking simply means that teachers and administrators examine and strive to create school and classroom conditions that are condu-

cive to children's thinking. This means that:

1. Teachers *pose problems, raise questions,* and intervene with paradoxes, dilemmas, and discrepancies that students can try to resolve.

2. Teachers and administrators *structure* the school environment for thinking—value it, make time for it, secure support materials, and evaluate growth in it.

3. Teachers and administrators *respond* to students' ideas in such a way as to maintain a school and classroom climate that creates trust, allows risktaking, and is experimental, creative, and positive. This requires listening to students' and each other's ideas, remaining nonjudgmental, and having rich data sources.

4. Teachers, administrators, and other adults in the school environment *model* the behaviors of

thinking that are desired in students.

Accomplishing all of the above would go far in encouraging students to use their native intelligence. However, there's more. Students haven't learned to think yet.

Teaching OF Thinking

Most authors and developers of major cognitive curriculum projects agree that direct instruction in thinking skills is imperative. Beyer, de Bono, Feuerstein, Lipman, and Whimbey would probably agree on at least one point: the teaching of thinking requires teachers to instruct students directly in the processes of thinking. Even Perkins believes that creativity can be taught—by design.

This does not mean that a curriculum program must be purchased, inserviced, and installed. While this is surely a viable option, and should be considered, there are other ways of teaching students thinking skills: analyzing the subject areas or skills being taught in the normal curriculum for their prerequisite cognitive abilities and then teaching those skills directly, for example. The act of decoding in reading requires analysis, comparison, making analogies, inferring, synthesizing, and evaluating. Teaching of thinking, therefore, means that these cognitive skills are taught *directly* as part of the reading (decoding) program.

Critical thinking skills might be taught directly during a social studies unit on the election process. Steps in problem solving might be taught directly during math and science instruction. The qualities of fluency and metaphorical thinking might be taught directly during creative writing, and so forth. Creating conditions for thinking and teaching it directly are excellent procedures, but what about the application? Nothing yet has been taught about the transference of these thinking skills beyond the context in which they were learned. Students may be able to identify the steps in the problem-solving process and correctly distinguish between classification and categorization, but do they have any inclination to use these skills in real-life situations? There's more.

Teaching ABOUT Thinking

Teaching about thinking can be divided into at least three components: brain functioning, metacognition, and epistemic cognition.

1. *Brain functioning.* Recently neurobiological research has shed light on how our brains work. Teaching about thinking would include investigating such curiosities as: How do we think? How does memory work? What causes emotions? Why do we dream? How do we learn? How and why do mental disorders occur? What happens when part of the brain is damaged? Restak's *The Brain,* Ornstein and Thompson's *The Amazing Brain,* and Russell's *The*

Figure 1	Staff Development Matrix for Thinking Skills		
Levels of Skill Development	**I. Teaching For Thinking:** Creating school and classroom conditions conducive to full cognitive development	**II. Teaching Of Thinking:** Instructing students in the skills and strategies directly or implementing one or more programs	**III. Teaching About Thinking:** Helping students become aware of their own and others' cognitive processes and their use in real-life situations and problems
A. Awareness Developed by lectures, readings, witnessing demonstrations, etc.	**I A**	**II A**	**III A**
B. Knowledge and Comprehension Developed by modeling, practicing, comparing, discussing, interacting	**I B**	**II B**	**III B**
C. Mastery of Skills Developed by practicing with feedback and coaching	**I C**	**II C**	**III C**
D. Application Developed by extended use across subject areas, varieties of groups, demonstrations; critique and dialogue with others	**I D**	**II D**	**III D**
E. Trainer of Trainers Developed by creating, conducting, and critiquing inservice strategies; observing the training of other trainers	**I E**	**II E**	**III E**

Brain Book are sources of information. A recent public television series entitled "The Brain" has heightened this awareness and is available for use in schools.

2. *Metacognition.* Being conscious of our own thinking and problem solving while thinking is known as metacognition. It is a uniquely human ability occurring in the neocortex of the brain. Good problem solvers plan a course of action before they begin a task, monitor themselves while executing that plan, back up or adjust the plan consciously, and evaluate themselves upon completion.

Metacognition in the classroom might be characterized by having discussions with students about what is going on inside their heads while they're thinking; comparing different students' approaches to problem solving and decision making; identifying what is known, what needs to be known, and how to produce that knowledge; or having students think aloud while problem solving.

Metacognitive instruction would include learning how to learn; how to study for a test; how to use strategies of question asking before, during, and after reading. It might include knowing how to learn best—visually, auditorily, kinesthetically—and what strategies to use when you find yourself in a situation that does *not* match your best learning modality.

Metacognition is discussed more extensively later in this book. See also Costa (1984).

3. *Epistemic cognition.* Epistemology is the study of how knowledge is produced. In the curriculum it might include studying the lives, processes, and works of great composers, artists, scientists, and philosophers. Epistemological questions for discussion include:

- How does what scientists do differ from what artists do?

- What are the procedures of inquiry used by anthropologists as they live with and study a culture?

- What goes on inside a maestro's mind as he or she conducts an orchestra?

- What was it about Mozart's genius that allowed him to "hear" a total musical composition before writing it down?

- What process do poets use to create?

- Why can't we use processes of scientific inquiry to solve social problems?

Epistemic cognition is the study and comparison of great artists, scientists, and scholars and the differential processes of investigation, inquiry, and creativity that underlie their productivity. Lipman's Philosophy for Children program is especially well-suited for this. Other resources include Perkins' *The Mind's Best Work*, Madigan and Elwood's *Brainstorms and Thunderbolts: How Creative Genius Works*, and Gardner's *Art, Mind, and Brain.*

Installing A Program For Thinking

Installing a program of teaching for thinking does not happen overnight. It takes time, patience, and practice. Joyce and others have created a helpful paradigm for thinking about the steps and sequences in staff development efforts. They suggest a series of stages and levels of concern through which teachers proceed during the change process. Their

38

Figure 2	I. Teaching FOR Thinking
Intersection	**Competencies of Teachers**
I A	Is aware of different levels of questions and various ways of organizing the classroom for instruction. Can describe alternative ways of responding so as to maintain and extend students' thinking.
I B	Plans lessons to incorporate levels of questions, response behaviors, and classroom organization for thinking. Seeks assistance, advice from others in methods and materials for teaching thinking.
I C	Invites others to observe a lesson, then to give feedback about questioning skills, classroom organization, and response behaviors. Volunteers to do the same for colleagues.
I D	Incorporates thinking skills across subject areas. Devotes maximum time to teaching for thinking. Shares ideas and materials with colleagues. Strives to model rational thinking processes in own behavior.
I E	Conducts inservice for colleagues. Videotapes own lessons and shares with colleagues. Plans, conducts, and evaluates staff development strategies. Analyzes school and classroom conditions for their conduciveness to and modeling of thinking. Works to improve them.

Figure 3	II. Teaching OF Thinking
Intersection	**Competencies of Teachers**
II A	Is aware of various programs intended to teach thinking directly. Is aware of definitions and distinctions among various thinking skills and strategies.
II B	Employs lessons intended to directly teach thinking skills. Incorporates thinking skills into content areas. Attends training in a curriculum program intended to teach thinking directly.
II C	Invites others to observe and give feedback about lessons in which thinking is taught directly. Applies knowledge learned in training programs to instruction. Devotes two to three hours per week to teaching thinking directly.
II D	Distinguishes among several major curriculums intended to teach thinking. Diagnoses students' cognitive deficiencies and provides experiences to remediate them. Analyzes the cognitive skills prerequisite for students to master school subjects, and incorporates instruction in those skills.
II E	Develops and implements inservice training in one or more of the major curriculum programs. Trains others in the development of lesson plans incorporating direct instruction of thinking skills and strategies. Surveys and recommends adoption of instructional materials that enhance thinking skills.

Figure 4

III. Teaching ABOUT Thinking

Intersection	Competencies of Teachers
III A	Is aware of differences in modality strengths, learning styles, and brain functioning. Can define such terms as metacognition and epistemology.
III B	Attempts metacognitive discussions with students. Discusses how the brain works. Selects materials on brain functioning and biographies of famous scientists and artists in an attempt to intrigue students.
III C	Invites colleagues to observe a lesson involving a philosophical/espistemological discussion and seeks feedback as to ways to improve. Reads and attends courses and lectures, watches video programs on philosophy, cognition, brain functioning, and so on. Discusses differences in learning strengths and modalities with students.
III D	Selects materials and conducts lessons in which comparisons are made of strategic reasoning, knowledge production, and creativity. Discusses with students such topics as artificial intelligence, the analysis of propaganda, and strategies of learning. Models metacognition overtly in the presence of students.
III E	Develops, conducts, and evaluates inservice strategies for colleagues for instruction on brain functioning, learning style differences, and metacognition. Develops curriculum incorporating materials and learning activities intended to have students learn to think and learn about thinking. Designs assessment tools and techniques to gather evidence of students' growth in intelligent behaviors.

procedure includes inservice techniques that help teachers raise their skill development levels in using new skills and behaviors.

The matrix for staff development presented in Figure 1 combines two components—*teaching for, of, and about thinking* and the *levels of skill development.* Figures, 2, 3, and 4 provide examples of teacher competencies, skills, and knowledge as educators of what might be included at each intersection in the matrix. Please consider these examples merely as helpful starting points to which you can add your own indicators of competence.

References

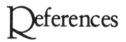

Costa, A. "Mediating the Metacognitive." *Educational Leadership* 42 (November 1984): 57-62.

Gardner, H. *Art, Mind, and Brain.* New York: Basic Books, 1982.

Hart, L. *Human Brain and Human Learning.* New York: Longman, 1975.

Madigan, C. and Elwood, A. *Brainstorms and Thunderbolts: How Creative Genius Works.* New York: Macmillan, 1983.

Perkins, D. *The Mind's Best Work.*
Cambridge: Harvard University Press,
1981.

Restak, R. *The Brain: The Last Frontier.*
New York: Warner Books, 1979.

Russell, P. *The Brain Book.* New York: E.
P. Dutton, 1979.

——— ❧ ———

5

Teacher-Initiated Questions And Directions That Elicit Thinking And Learning

Learning and memory are influenced by the sets, intentions, and plans generated in the neocortex of the brain, as well as by the information received from the immediate environment and from internal states, drives, and muscular responses. The reality we perceive, feel, see, and hear is influenced by the constructive process of the brain, as well as by the cues that impinge upon it.

—Merlin C. Wittrock, 1978

The information processing model described in this chapter serves as a basis for the definitions of thinking, instructional strategies, and teaching behaviors discussed in later chapters. Such a model serves as a guide to curriculum and instructional development, *not* as a neurobiological definition of thinking. Such a definition is still open to interpretation. In fact, brain researchers are attempting to discover whether thinking is a natural bodily function similar to the heart pumping blood or whether it is the result of intense effort, strict discipline, and careful programming of instructional outcomes.

While there are numerous models of human intellectual functioning, it is best to adopt a familiar one as a guide. For example, if you're familiar with Bloom's Taxonomy (Bloom 1956) or Guilford's Structure of the Intellect (Guilford 1967), you can use them as a guide in materials selection, staff development, and defining thinking. Adopting a description of human intellectual functioning can help you recognize and develop teaching methodologies, curriculum sequences, learning activities, and assessment procedures that go beyond superficial learning.

An examination of several models of thinking yields more similarities than differences. Many authors distinguish three to four basic thought clusters (Smith and Tyler 1945): (1) *input* of data through the senses and from memory; (2) *processing* those data into meaningful relationships; (3) *output* or application of those relationships in new or novel situations; and (4) *metacognition.* Figure 1 presents a comparison of several authors' constructs.

Thinking is the receiving of external stimuli through the senses followed by internal processing. If the new information should be stored, the brain attempts to match, compare, categorize, and pattern it with similar information already in storage. This process is done extremely quickly in an apparently random order, and either at the conscious or unconscious level.

Thus, every event a person experiences causes the brain to call up meaningful, related information from storage—whether the event is commonplace or a carefully developed classroom learning experience. The more meaningful, relevant, and complex the experience is, the more actively the brain attempts to integrate

Figure 1	**Comparison of Thinking Models**		
Data Input Phase	**Processing Phase**	**Output Phase**	**Source**
Internal and external input	Central Processing	Output	Atkinson & Shiffrin, 1968, pp. 90-122
Participation and awareness	Internalization	Dissemination	Bell & Steinaker, 1979
Knowledge	Comprehension Analysis Synthesis	Application Evaluation	Bloom & others, 1956
Descriptive	Interpretive	Evaluative	Eisner, 1979, pp. 203-213; Great Books Foundation
Input	Elaboration	Output	Feuerstein, 1980, pp. 71-103
Fluency	Manipulation	Persistence	Foshay, 1979, pp. 93-113
Cognition and memory	Evaluation	Convergent and divergent production	Guilford, 1967
Fact	Concept	Value	Harmin, 1973
Receiving	Responding Valuing Organizing	Characterizing	Krathwohl & others, 1964
Alertness	Information processing	Action	Restak, 1979, p. 44
Learning	Integrating	Applying	Sexton & Poling, 1973, p. 7
Intuitive	Awareness	Function	Strasser & others, 1972, pp. 46-47
Intake storage	Mediation	Action	Suchman, 1966, pp. 177-187
Concept formation	Interpretation Inference	Application	Taba, 1964, pp. 30-38
Detailed information recall of previous knowledge	Comparison	Rule generation Auto-criticism	Whimbey, 1976, pp. 116-138
Pre-exposure	Exposure	Re-creation	Barazakov, 1984

From *Toward a Model of Human Intellectual Functioning*

and assimilate it into its existing storehouse of programs and structures. According to this model of intellectual functioning, the most complex thinking occurs when external stimuli challenge the brain to (1) draw upon the greatest amount of data or structures already in storage; (2) expand an already existing structure; and (3) develop new structures.

A problem may be defined as any stimulus or challenge, the response to which is not readily apparent. If there is a ready match between what is perceived by the senses and what is an existing structure or program already in storage, no problem exists. Piaget calls this *assimilation*. If, however, the new information cannot be explained or resolved with knowledge in short- or long-term memory, the information must be processed, action taken to gather more information to resolve the discrepancy, and the ultimate resolution evaluated for its "fit" with reality. Piaget refers to this as *accommodation*. Our brains seem to dislike disequilibrium and constantly strive to satisfy and resolve discrepancies perceived in the environment.

Inputting information alone seems to be brain-dysfunctional. Information that the brain has not processed remains in memory for very short periods of time. Merely experiencing or memorizing without acting on that information commits it to short-term memory. Finding a pattern through

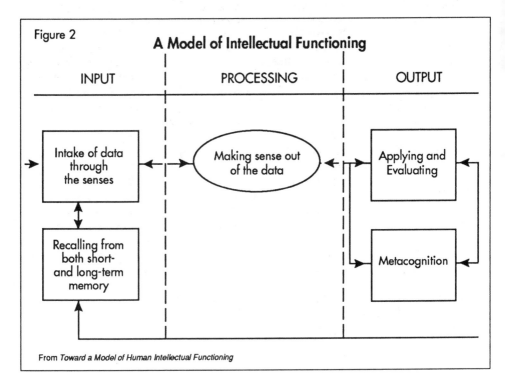

Figure 2

A Model of Intellectual Functioning

INPUT | PROCESSING | OUTPUT

Intake of data through the senses

Making sense out of the data

Applying and Evaluating

Recalling from both short- and long-term memory

Metacognition

From *Toward a Model of Human Intellectual Functioning*

comparisons, classifications, and causal, sequential, or hierarchical relationships apparently forms or expands a structure in the brain so that the information is available for application in situations other than that in which it was learned. For example, try to remember which direction Lincoln, Kennedy, Roosevelt, and Jefferson are facing on their respective coins. Only when comparisons are made, relationships drawn, and connections built will this information stay in long-term memory.

Figure 2 provides a simplistic visual presentation of this complex model of intellectual functioning. It deletes such important factors as affect, motivation, and perceptual abilities.

Our brains never stop. We process information during sleep and even under anesthesia. The brain actively engages in these processes regardless of the external input that is presented. The brain does *not* remain inactive when it is not fully engaged in learning specific information. When learning tasks are presented that are insufficiently organized, unmotivating, or are not meaningful enough to engage these thought processes, the brain seeks stimulation in other ways: random thoughts, feelings, physical sensations, daydreaming, fantasy, problem solving, creative inspiration, and spontaneous memories. Instead of focusing on a lecture on igneous, sedimentary, and metamorphic rocks, for example, the brain may focus on

the teacher's blue dress and start daydreaming about what to wear to the dance next Saturday. Thus, the brain continues to find patterns and relationships but not necessarily in the direction that the teacher intends.

Teachers and parents are crucial mediators of these intellectual behaviors. They can present or call attention to discrepancies and pose problems intended to invite more than a memory (assimilation) type response. Teachers can arrange the classroom and learning experiences to cause the exercise of these intellectual functions.

Teachers' Questions and Statements That Cause Thinking

Early in their school experience, children learn to listen and respond to the language of the teacher. From questions and other statements that the teacher poses, students derive their cues for expected behavior. Questions are the intellectual tools by which teachers most often elicit the desired behavior of their students. Thus, they can use questions to elicit certain cognitive objectives or thinking skills. Embedded in questions and other statements are the cues for the cognitive task or behavior the student is to perform (Davis and Tinsley 1967).

There is a relationship between the level of thinking inherent in teachers' verbal behavior and the level of thinking of their students (Measel and Mood 1972). Correlations have been found between the syntax of the teacher's questions and the syntax of the student's response (Cole and Williams 1973). Furthermore, teachers whose questions more frequently require divergent thinking produce more divergent thinking on the part of their students, in contrast to teachers who use more cognitive memory questions (Gallagher and Ashner 1963). Students score higher on tests of critical thinking and on standardized achievement tests when teachers use higher-level questions (Newton 1978; Redfield and Rousseau 1981).

Realizing that teachers can cause students to think by carefully designing the syntax of questions and other statements, let us now return to the Model of Intellectual Functioning [see Figure 2]. This model will serve as a basis for the composition of questions. Teachers can cause students to perform the intellectual functions represented in this model by composing questions and other statements with certain syntactical arrangements.

Thus, with a model of intellectual functioning in mind, the teacher can manipulate the syntactical structure of questions and other statements to invite students to accept information, to process or compare that information with what they already know, to draw meaningful relationships, and to apply or transfer those relationships to hypothetical or novel situations.

The following sections provide examples of questions or statements that the teacher might pose to cause students to take in information— through the senses or from memory; to process that information; and to apply, transfer, or evaluate relationships in new or hypothetical situations.

Gathering and Recalling Information (Input)

To cause the student to *input* data, the teacher can design questions and statements to draw from the student the concepts, information, feelings, or experiences acquired in the past and stored in long- or short-term memory. Questions can also be designed to activate the senses to gather data that students can then process at the next higher level. There are several cognitive processes included at the *input* level of thinking. Some verbs that may serve as predicates of behavioral objective statements are: completing, counting, matching, naming, defining, observing, reciting, selecting, describing, listing, identifying, and recalling.

Examples of questions or statements designed to elicit these cognitive objectives are:

Question/Statement	Desired Cognitive Behavior
Name the states that bound California	*Naming*

Question/Statement	Desired Cognitive Behavior
How does this picture make you feel?	*Describing*
What word does this picture go with?	*Matching*
What were the names of the children in the story?	*Naming*
How many coins are in the stack?	*Counting*
Which words on this list are rhyming words?	*Selecting*
Mexican houses were made of mud bricks called_____.	*Completing*
List the four numbers in a set of positive integers.	*Listing*
How did you feel about the grade you received in algebra?	*Recalling*

Making Sense of Gathered Information (Processing)

To help students process the data gathered through the senses and retrieved from long- and short-term memory, teachers' questions and statements should prompt students to draw relationships of cause and effect, to synthesize, analyze, summarize, compare, contrast, or classify the data they have acquired or observed. Following are some verbs that may serve as the predicates of behavioral objective statements if the desired cognitive behavior is at the processing level: synthesizing, analyzing, categorizing, explaining, classifying, comparing, contrasting, stating causality, inferring, experimenting, organizing, distinguishing, sequencing, summarizing, grouping, and making analogies.

Examples of questions or statements designed to elicit these cognitive objectives are:

Question/Statement	Desired Cognitive Behavior
Why did Columbus believe he could get to the east by sailing west?	*Explaining*
What do you think caused the liquid to turn blue?	*Stating causality*
What other machines can you think of that work on the same principle as this one?	*Making analogies*
How can you arrange the blocks to give a crowded feeling?	*Organizing*
How are pine needles different from redwood needles?	*Contrasting*
How does the formula	*Comparing*

for finding the volume of a cone compare with the formula for finding the volume of a pyramid?

Arrange the following elements of a set in ascending order: 13/4, 3/2, 5/6, 32/5. *Sequencing*

From our experiments with food coloring in different water temperatures, what can you infer about the movement of molecules? *Inferring*

Applying and Evaluating Actions in Novel Situations (Output)

Questions and statements that lead to *output* require students to go beyond the concepts or principles they have developed and to use this relationship in novel or hypothetical situations. Application invites students to think creatively and hypothetically, to use imagination, to expose or apply value systems, or to make judgments. Following are some verbs that may serve as predicates for behavioral objective statements if the desired cognitive behavior of students is at the application level: applying a principle, imagining, planning, evaluating, judging, predicting, extrapolating, creating, forecasting, inventing, hypothesizing, speculating, generalizing, model building, and designing.

Examples of questions designed to elicit these cognitive objectives are:

Question	Desired Cognitive Behavior
If our population continues to grow as it has been, what will life be like in the 21st Century?	*Speculating*
What can you say about all countries' economies that are dependent on only one crop?	*Generalizing*
What would be the fairest solution to this problem?	*Evaluating*
From what we have learned, which painting is the best example of modern art?	*Judging*
What do you think might happen if we placed the saltwater fish in the freshwater aquarium?	*Hypothesizing*

Teachers have awesome power. Through the careful and selective use of questions and other statements, they can elicit and invite intelligent behavior.

49

eferences

Atkinson, R.C. and Siffrin, R. M. "Human Memory: A Proposed System and Its Control Process." In *The Psychology of Learning and Motivation.* Vol. 2. Edited by K. W. Spence and J. T. Spence. New York: Academic Press, 1968.

Bell, M. and Steinaker, N. *The Experiential Taxonomy: A New Approach to Teaching and Learning.* New York: Academic Press, 1979.

Bloom, B. S.; Engelhart, M. D.; Furst, E. J.; Hill, W. H; and Krathwohl, D. R. *Taxonomy of Educational Objectives: Handbook I: Cognitive Domain.* New York: David McKay, 1956.

Cole, R.A. and Williams, D. "Pupil Responses to Teacher Questions: Cognitive Level, Length, and Syntax." In *Educational Leadership* 31, 1973.

Davis, O.L. and Tinsley, D. "Cognitive Objectives Revealed by Classroom Questions Asked by Social Studies Teachers." *Peabody Journal of Education* 45.

Eisner, E. *The Educational Imagination.* New York: Macmillan, 1979.

Feuerstein, R. *Instrumental Enrichment.* Baltimore: University Park Press, 1980.

Foshay, A. W. "Toward a Humane Curriculum." In *Education in Flux: Implications for Curriculum Development.* Edited by J. J. Jelenek. Tempe: University of Arizona Press, 1979.

Gallagher, J. and Ashner, M.J. "A Preliminary Report: Analysis of Classroom Interaction." *Merill Palmer Quarterly* 9, 1963.

Guilford, J. P. *The Nature of Human Intelligence.* New York: McGraw-Hill, 1967.

Harmin, M.; Kirschenbaum, H.; and Simon, S. *Clarifying Values Through Subject Matter.* Minneapolis: Winston Press, Inc., 1973.

Krathwohl, D.; Bloom, B. S.; and Masia, B. B. *Taxonomy of Educational Objectives: Handbook II: Affective Domain.* New York: David McKay, 1964.

Measel, W. and Mood, D. "Teacher Verbal Behavior and Teacher and Pupil Thinking in Elementary School." In *Journal of Educational Research* 66, 1972.

Newton, B. "Theoretical Basis for Higher Cognitive Questioning—An Avenue to Critical Thinking." In *Education* 98, 1978.

Redfield, D. and Rousseau, E. "A Meta-Analysis on Teacher Questioning Behavior." In *Review of Educational Research* 51, 1981.

Restak, R. *The Brain: The Last Frontier.* New York: Warner Books, 1979.

Sexton, T. G. and Poling, D. R. *Can Intelligence Be Taught?* Bloomington, IN: Phi Delta Kappa Educational Foundation Fastbook Series #29, 1973.

Smith, E. R. and Tyler, R. W. *Appraising and Recording Student Progress.* New York: Harper, 1942.

Strasser, B. B.; Babcock, R. W.; Cowan, R.; Dalis, G. T.; Gothold, S. E.; and Rudolph, J. R. *Teaching Toward Inquiry.* Washington, D.C.: National Education Association, 1972.

Suchman, J. R. "A Model for the Analysis of Inquiry." In *Analyses of Concept Learning.* New York: Academic Press, Inc., 1966.

Taba, H.; Levine, S.; and Elzey, E. *Thinking in Elementary School Children.* San Francisco: San Francisco State College, Cooperative Research Project No. 1574, 1964.

Whimbey, A. and Whimbey, L. S. *Intelligence Can Be Taught.* New York: Bantam Books, 1976.

Wittrock, Merlin C. In *Cognitive Processes of the Brain, 1978 Yearbook of the National Society for the Study of Education, Part II.* NSSE, 1978.

——— ‌❧ ———

Teacher Response Behaviors That Support And Extend Thinking And Learning

Teacher: "How do you think our country would have developed differently had the early explorers landed on the West Coast and moved east across our country rather than landing on the East Coast and moving west across our country—an eastward movement rather than a westward movement?"

Student A: "Our laws would be different."

Teacher: "No."

Student B: "Our language might be different."

Teacher: "No."

Student C: "It would have taken longer to populate our country because of the mountains and deserts would have kept the settlers on the West Coast longer. "

Teacher: "Yes, good for you."

In the above example, how has the teacher's response to students' ideas inhibited or extended students' thinking? How would you have felt if your idea was discredited, put down, or ignored? How would you feel toward other students whose ideas were praised and valued while yours were criticized?

The manner in which teachers respond to students has great influence on the student. Lowery (1980) found that the way teachers respond has greater influence on students' thinking than what the teacher asks or tells them to do. Students are constantly anticipating how their teacher will respond to their actions. Thus, the way teachers respond to students seems to exert greater influence than the teachers' questioning. It has also been found that the teachers' responses have a great deal of influence on the development of students' self-concept, their attitude toward learning, their achievement, and their classroom rapport.

What Are Teacher Response Behaviors?

Response behaviors may be categorized according to the effect those behaviors have on students: those that tend to terminate or close down thinking, and those that maintain, open up, or extend thinking. There are six behaviors that can be classified under these two categories.

Terminal or closed responses:

1. Criticizing (and other put-downs)

2. Praising

Open or extending responses:

1. Using silence (wait time)

2. Accepting—passively, actively, or empathetically

3. Clarifying—of both concept and process

4. Facilitating data acquisition

   Much research accumulated over several years supports the beneficial effects on students when teachers use these behaviors in the manner suggested here. Descriptions and explanations of each behavior and the research supporting its use are presented on the following pages.

Terminal Or Closed Responses

1. Criticizing (and other put-downs)

Criticism may be defined as negative value judgments. When a teacher responds to a student's ideas or actions with such negative words as "poor," "incorrect," or wrong," the response tends to signal inadequacy or disapproval and terminates the student's thinking about the task. Negative responses can sometimes be subtle, such as "You're *almost* right," or "Who has a *better* answer?" or "You're getting *close.*" Sometimes negative responses take the form of ridicule: "What a dumb idea," or "You're not good enough." Other times they are sarcastic and may involve negative inflections: "Who would want to help you when you act *that* way?" "Where on earth did you get *that* idea?" "Now that Mary is finished, who will show us the way it *should* be done?"

   An abundance of research has found that the use of criticism is not helpful in promoting learning (Soar 1972). When teachers respond to students, criticism produces negative pupil attitudes and lower pupil achievement.

   The use of criticism, therefore, is *not* an appropriate way for a teacher to respond since it leaves the student with a feeling of failure, cognitive inadequacy, and poor self-concept. It neither encourages nor enhances thinking.

2. Praising

Praise may be defined as the opposite of criticism in that it employs the use of positive value judgments such as "good," "excellent," "great," and so on. Following are some examples of teacher responses that use praise:

"That was a very *good* answer, Linda."

"Your painting is *excellent.*"

"You're such a *fine* boy today, Leo."

"Yours was the *best* example that anybody gave."

Surprisingly, while many teachers advocate the use of praise in attempts to reinforce behaviors and to build self-worth, the research on praise indicates that the opposite is more often the case. Praise builds conformity. It makes students depend on others for their worth rather than upon themselves. It has been found to be a detriment to creativity (Kohn 1987).

Some teachers use praise so often and so indiscriminately that it becomes a meaningless response, and students derive little benefit from it. Praise is appropriate under certain conditions described below. It would be desirable for teachers to learn to recognize and use praise sparingly and judiciously and only in those circumstances, with only those students, and for only those objectives for which it is suitable. It is also desirable that teachers replace praising with an enlarged repertoire of response behaviors that research indicates are more conducive to developing students' thinking skills.

Praising seems best used with only certain students and for certain tasks. Following are three circumstances in which praise seems warranted:

a. *With reluctant, unmotivated, dependent learners*
Some students are difficult to motivate. They are highly dependent upon the teacher for reinforcement and need constant reminders to stay on task. These are often students who, when given an assignment soon lose interest, have a limited attention span, and quickly seek redirection. While praise often benefits this type of learner, a goal for them should be to replace external reinforcement with internal motivation. Therefore, the amount and frequency of praise must gradually be reduced and replaced with the satisfaction derived from solving intriguing problems, accuracy and craftsmanship of tasks completed, and responsibility for contributing to group accomplishment. Thus, with this type of learner, the teacher must consciously withdraw praise over time (fading). Often when new or difficult learning is begun, praise will need to be used again briefly until the student has a feeling of confidence and mastery.

b. *With lower grade level students*
Lawrence Kohlberg (1978) has

described a sequence through which students grow in their understanding of social justice and moral reasoning. During early stages, children "understand" right and wrong because of the "rewards and punishments" given by adults and others in authority. These rewards and punishments are the consequences of their behavior. In later life, students can understand the consequences of their behavior because of their effect on others or because they understand what is "morally ethical" behavior. While students are still in the early stages of moral development, praise and rewards may be appropriate. These stages are not necessarily determined by chronological maturity, but rather by observation of students' behavior in situations requiring social decision making and by analyzing discussions with children about appropriate behavior in varying problem situations. Higher levels, more autonomous, more appropriate, kinder, and more just behaviors will develop in students if they are involved in decisions and problem situations that require making a choice of behaviors. It is helpful if their behaviors are discussed and analyzed with them, and if significant adults in their environment model those more appropriate social behaviors.

While praise may seem to be more appropriate with young, morally immature students, we want to help them progress beyond that stage. Teachers, therefore, must soon abolish praising and replace it with the type of internal motivation system which is consistent with the higher stages of moral development.

c. Low-level cognitive tasks

Input or knowledge level questions are used for the purpose of having students confirm or produce an answer from memory or from sensory observations. It is probable that the answer the student gives is predictable and therefore "correct." The teacher's response to the student's answer to an input question may warrant validation. For example:

Teacher: "What is the largest city in California?"

Student: "San Francisco?"

Teacher: "No, Jane, not San Francisco."

Student: "Los Angeles?"

Teacher: "Yes, Bill, that's correct. Los Angeles is the largest."

Some guidelines for using praise

If praise is used, there are some guidelines that can help students decrease their dependence on it.

a. *Giving the criteria or rationale for the value judgment*

If praise is given, it is important that the criteria for the praise be described. What makes an act "good," or "excellent," must be communicated along with the praise. Thereby, the student understands the reason or criteria that makes the act acceptable and thus that performance can be repeated.

b. *Helping students analyze their own answer*

Teacher: "Jane says San Francisco is the largest city in California. Bill says Los Angeles is the largest. Would each of you please tell us what is the population of the two cities? One way to find out is to compare our data."

This discussion has been an attempt to describe the strengths and limitations of the use of the terminal response behaviors: criticizing and praising. The few conditions in which praising or giving positive value judgments seems appropriate have been described. It is intended that the use of these terminal behaviors be *decreased* and that other alternative response behaviors which have a more instructive effect on students' cognitive development be *increased*. These alternatives will be discussed later.

Most teachers enjoy rewarding and praising their students. Brophy (1981), however, found that the one person in the classroom for whom praise has the most beneficial effect is, indeed, the

teacher. It is understandable, therefore, that research studies showing the detrimental effects of rewards are met with resistance.

While some rewards and praise may be warranted, the research indicates that there are other instructional situations in which they are not. The judicious use of praise seems to depend upon discriminating: 1). What kind of learners need it? 2). Which instructional goals and objectives warrant it?

Such learning variables as interest, motivation, achievement, perseverance, creativity, and internal locus of control are all adversely affected when the teacher uses praise and rewards.

When teachers reduce verbal rewarding children demand less time for "showing and telling." They then increase comparison and discussion leading to experimentation. There is also an increase in speculation. When praise and rewards are given, they tend to inhibit experimentation (Rowe 1974).

It has also been found that high use of praise affects the sociometrics of the classroom. Students receiving praise from the teacher are more often selected by their classmates as the ones most desired to be with and work with. In those classrooms where praise was withheld, a more diffused sociometric pattern resulted; greater numbers of students, rather than a few "stars," were selected workmates (Daily 1970).

Much teacher praise is associated with lower pupil nonverbal creativity (Kohn 1987). Reinforcement through the use of such comments as "uh-huh" and "okay" was positively related to some achievement scores, while frequent use of stronger praise is not (Wallen and Woodke 1963).

While teachers may have good intentions in using praise or rewards, what is more important is how the student interprets it. That determines whether the reward will have its intended effect. Teachers must be sensitive to individual student's interpretation of rewards and praise and will therefore, choose to praise or reward according to the timing, circumstances, and type of rewards and praise to be given.

What type of learner needs praise?

If motivation is already in evidence when the student is already engaged in the desired behaviors, rewards can be counter-productive. Rather than reinforcing the enthusiasm that is present and increasing the student's motivation, the additional praise actually reduces it.

Unfortunately, many students lack motivation. Some teachers use rewards as a means of instilling motivation. Rewards, however, are not the answer to these conditions either. Joyce and Showers (1988, p. 56) state: "Praise and rewards, which are often associated with moderate class mean gains, were *negatively* correlated with both high and low achievers." Using rewards and praise as motivators of student learning increases the student's dependency on others for learning rather than finding the learning inherently satisfying or involving the acquisition or exercise of skills which the students value themselves (Lepper and Green 1978).

Younger children may need more praise than older children. In kindergarten through second or even third grades, most children are compliant and oriented toward conforming to and pleasing their teachers. They are learning classroom and school rules, procedures, and routines, as well as how to function as a member of a group. Praise and rewards seem appropriate in the socialization process at an early grade level. As children mature, however, from about grades two to three and beyond, they have learned what they need to know about school and classroom routines and procedures and less and less time needs to be spent on such conformity. Where a first grade boy might be delighted when his teacher points out his behavior, the same boy in the fifth grade would be horrified if the teacher said, "I like the way John is sitting nice and tall, ready to begin work."

Which instructional objectives warrant praise?

Flanders (1970) stated:

"The pupil growth index, which involves memory, a relatively low-level cognitive task, can tolerate lower levels of teacher indirectness.... Yet higher levels of cognitive reasoning are associated with more indirect...teacher influence patterns: creativity appears to flourish most with the most indirect patterns."

Student performance on routine, familiar procedures is not adversely affected by rewards and praise. In fact, when students do not particularly like assignments that are repetitious and of a practice nature, rewards seem to enhance their performance. On the other hand, rewards have a detrimental effect on student performance on tasks requiring higher-level problem solving. The learning *process* is different from the learning *product*. The process is detrimentally affected by rewards. The effects of rewards differ depending on the extent to which the student has already learned the subject matter. Thus, rewards for tasks already learned are not detrimental because the process of learning had already occurred and the focus is now on learner production of what he or she already knows.

In contrast, the *process* of learning *is* detrimentally affected by rewards. The performance of learning new tasks, skills, and processes requires cognitive risks and exploration which is inhibited by praise and promised reward. Evidently rewards are best administered in well-learned tasks where specific rules need to be followed as opposed to learnings which are in the process of being learned or are problem-solving/exploratory in nature. Seatwork, which is of a practice nature, is likely to be facilitated by rewards, while rewards for students learning a new skill are likely to have a detrimental effect.

Open Or Extending Responses

1. Using Silence

Many teachers wait only one or two seconds after having asked a question before they either call on another student, ask another question, or give the answer to the question themselves. Many teachers feel that unless someone is talking, no one is learning. If the teacher waits after asking a question, or after a student gives an answer, there is an effect on students' cognitive behavior.

Sometimes periods of silence may seem interminably long. If, however, students are to be given opportunities to do their own thinking, their own reflecting, their own problem solving and determining an answer's appropriateness, then teachers need to be comfortable in allowing these periods of silence to occur.

If the teacher waits after asking a question, or after a student gives an answer, there are observable differences in classroom behaviors of students. If the teacher waits only a short time—one or two seconds—then short, one-word type of student responses will result. On the other hand, if the teacher waits for longer periods, the students tend to respond in whole sentences and complete thoughts. There is a perceptible increase in the creativity of the response as shown by greater use of descriptive and modifying words. There is also increased speculativeness in the student's thinking. Research has also shown that the student-to-student interaction is greater, the number of questions students ask increases, and previously shy students begin to contribute (Rowe 1974).

Teachers communicate expectancies of students through the use of silence. When the teacher asks a question and then waits for a student's answer, it demonstrates that the teacher not only expects an answer but also that the teacher has faith in the student's ability to answer it given enough time. If the teacher asks a question and then waits only a short time, then gives the answer him or herself, or calls on another student, or gives a hint, or seeks help from another student, it demonstrates that the student really can't answer the question and is considered too poor a student to offer an answer or to be able to reason for him/herself.

When the teacher waits after the student gives an answer, it causes the student to continue thinking about the task or question. When a teacher waits after the student asks a question, it models for the student thoughtfulness, reflectiveness, and restraint of impulsivity of the teacher—valued traits of effective thinkers.

2. Accepting Responses

Teachers who are non-evaluative and non-judgmental accept what students do. When they accept, they give no clues through posture, gesture, or word as to whether a student's idea, behavior, or feeling, is good, bad, better or worse, right or wrong. In response to a student's idea or action, acceptance of it provides a psychologically safe climate where the student can take risks, is entrusted with the responsibility of making decisions for himself, and can explore the consequences of his own actions. Acceptance provides conditions in which students are encouraged to examine and compare their own data, values, ideas, criteria, and feelings with those of others as well as those of the teacher. Even though these values and feelings may differ from those of the teacher, teachers can still accept these differences because they know that only the student is able to modify their own thinking.

While a teacher may respond by accepting in different ways, three types of accepting responses are described here: 1) Passive acceptance, 2) active acceptance, and 3) empathic acceptance.

a. Passive acceptance is a teacher response that simply receives and acknowledges, without value judgments, what the student says. It communicates that the student's ideas have been heard. Examples of this type of response are:

"Um-hmm," "That's one possibility," "Could be," or "I understand," (Passive, verbal accepting responses).

Nodding the head or recording without change, the student's statement on the chalkboard (Passive, non-verbal accepting responses).

b. Active acceptance is a teacher response that reflects what the students says or does by rephrasing, paraphrasing, recasting, translating, or summarizing. Teachers use this response when they want to extend, build upon, compare, or give an example based upon what the student has said. While the teacher may use different words than the student, the teacher strives to maintain the intent and accurate meaning of the student's idea. Active acceptance is more than passive acceptance because the teacher demonstrates not only that the student's message has been received but also that the message is understood.

Drawing on many supportive studies, Flanders (1970) stated:

"The percentage of teacher statements that make use of ideas and opinions previously expressed by pupils is directly related to average class scores on attitude scales of teacher attractiveness, liking the class, etc., as well as average achievement scores adjusted for initial ability. Attitude as well as language usage, social studies skills, arithmetic computation, and problem solving were correlated with the teacher behaviors which used or extended students' ideas. Achievement was high in classrooms where these behaviors were used."

Examples of this type of response are:

"Your explanation is that if the heat were increased, the molecules would move faster and therefore disperse the food coloring faster."

"I understand. Your idea is that we should all write our legislators rather than send them one letter from the group."

"Shawn's idea is that the leaves could be classified according to their shapes while Sarah's way is to group them by size."

"An example of what you mean was when we arranged our rock

collection according to several different classification systems."

c. Empathetic acceptance is a response that accepts feelings in addition to cognition. Teachers respond this way when they want to accept a student's feelings, emotions, or behaviors. Often teachers show empathy when they express similar feelings from their own experiences. Such responses communicate that the teacher not only "hears" the student's idea but also the emotions underlying the idea. Empathetic acceptance does not mean that the teacher condones acts of aggression or destructive behavior. Some examples of this type of response are:

"I can see why you're confused. Those directions are unclear to me, too."

"You're frustrated because you didn't get a chance to share your idea. We've all got to take turns and that requires patience. It's hard to wait when you're anxious to share."

The student enters the room and slams a math workbook on the desk. The teacher responds empathically to this behavior by saying: "Something must be upsetting you today. Did you have difficulty with that assignment?"

3. Clarifying

Clarifying is similar to accepting in that both behaviors reflect the teacher's concern for fully understanding the student's idea. While active acceptance demonstrates that the teacher *does* understand, *clarifying* means that the teacher *does not* understand what the student is saying and, therefore, more information is needed.

When a student uses some terminology, expresses a concept or idea, or asks a question that the teacher does not understand, the teacher may wish to clarify both the *content* of that idea and/or the *process* by which that idea was derived. The teacher may express a lack of understanding of the student's idea and seek further explanation of it. She/he may invite the student to become more specific by requesting the student to elaborate or rephrase the idea, or to seek descriptions of the thinking processes underlying the production of that idea.

The intent of clarifying is to help the teacher better understand the students' ideas, feelings, and thought processes (cognitive mapping). Clarifying is *not* a devious way of changing or redirecting what the student is thinking or feeling. It is not a way of directing the class' attention to the "correct answer."

Clarifying is often stated in the form of an interrogative but could also be a statement inviting further illumination. For example:

"Could you explain to us what you mean by 'charisma'?"

"What you are saying is that you'd rather work by yourself than in a group. Is that correct?"

"Go over that one more time, Shelley, I'm not sure I understand you."

"You say you are studying the situation. Tell us just exactly what you do when you 'study' something."

"Explain to us the steps you took to arrive at that answer."

By *clarifying*, teachers show the students that their ideas are worthy of exploration and consideration; the full meaning, however is not yet understood. Clarifying demonstrates that the teacher is interested in values, and wants to pursue students' thinking.

It has been found that when a teacher responds to students' comments by encouraging them to elaborate further, it has a positive effect on achievement. Students become more purposeful in their thinking and behaving.

4. Facilitating the Acquisition of Data

If one of the objectives of cognitive education is for students to process data by comparing, classifying, making inferences, or drawing causal relation-

ships, then data must be available for the student to process. Facilitating the acquisition of data means that when the teacher perceives the student needs information, or when the student requests additional information, the teacher provides it or makes it possible for the student to acquire the data, facts, or information needed or requested. Thus, it is classified as a response behavior.

The teacher, therefore, creates a climate that is responsive to the student's quest for information. Teachers do this in a variety of ways. Several ways teachers can facilitate data are as follows:

a. *By providing data (feedback) about a student's performance:*

"No, three times six is not twenty-four. Three times eight is twenty-four."

"Yes, you have spelled 'rhythm' correctly."

b. *By providing personal information or data (self-divulgence). (These are often in the form of "I" messages.):*

"I want you to know that chewing gum in this classroom really disturbs me."

"John, your pencil tapping is distracting me."

"The way you painted the tree makes me feel like I'm on the inside looking out."

c. *By making it possible for students to experiment with equipment and materials to find data or information for themselves:*

"Here's a larger test tube if you'd like to see how your experiment would turn out differently."

"We can see the film again if you want to check your observations."

d. *By making primary and secondary sources of information accessible:*

"Mary, this almanac gives information you will need for your report on the world's highest mountain ranges."

"Here's the dictionary. The best way to verify the spelling is to look it up."

e. *By responding to a student's request for information:*

Student: "What's this thing called?"

Teacher: "This piece of equipment is called a bell jar."

f. *By surveying the group for its feelings or for input of its information.*

"On this chart we have made a list of what you observed in the film.

We can keep this chart in front of us so that we can refer to it as we classify our observations."

"Let's go around the circle and share some of the feelings we had when we found out the school board decided to close our school."

g. *By labeling a thinking process or behavior:*

"That is an hypothesis you are posing, Gina."

"Sharing your crayons like that is an example of cooperation, Mark."

"The question you are asking is an attempt to verify the data."

Knowledge of results is the single most important variable governing the acquisition of skillful habits.

5. Distinctions between feedback and rewards

There is a difference between rewards and feedback. A teacher's response can either control one's behavior (rewards), or give information about one's competence (feedback). If a student perceives the teacher's reward as controlling, a decrease in the student's intrinsic motivation will likely occur. If the student perceives the reward as providing feedback about his or her knowledge or competence, however, an increase in intrinsic motivation is likely.

Feedback or response to a student's behavior needs to occur in a few seconds if learning is to progress rapidly. Feedback need not always come from the external situation but may arise from other concepts, data, and principles recalled or gathered by the learners themselves. For example, models may be provided to enable the student to check for accuracy or correctness, compare with other students' answers, or compare with rules stated in the instructions. In other words, the teacher needs to provide an opportunity for the student to perform an internal check of the ideas held with the data being gathered so that they can decide for themselves if the idea or answer is correct. This self-checking can furnish some immediate feedback and satisfaction that in turn reinforces learning.

Data of all kinds needs to be available in great abundance. It should be possible for the inquirer to obtain whatever data he or she wants as easily and quickly as possible from many sources: manipulation of materials, tools and references, the teacher, and other resource people.

concluded that the top concern of high school students was a lack of acceptance and involvement. Students felt no one cared and no one listened to their needs (Education USA, 1978).

Probably the main reason why all the open type of response behaviors described create the warm climate for learning is that they require teachers to listen. The teacher's use of silence communicates to students the teacher's value of reflective, thoughtful, crafted answers rather than impulsive answers. The use of accepting behaviors demands that teachers be sensitive to and understand students' ideas. They signal students that the product of their mind has meaning and influence to another human being. Clarifying and probing demonstrate a desire to go deeper and to further explore the power of the students' ideas. Facilitating data requires that teachers listen to and sense the students' need for information so that proper data may be supplied. Performance of all these behaviors presents a model of the type of rational behaviors that teachers desire in students as well.

In Summary

In a poll conducted by the University of Northern Colorado, 87% of the parents surveyed said the ability to communicate, understand, and relate was a very important quality that their children's teachers should have. The Colorado Department of Education

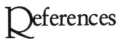

References

Brophy, J. E. "Teacher Praise: A Functional Analysis." East Lansing, MI: Michigan State University Institute for

Research on Teaching, October, 1981 (Occasional Paper No. 28).

Daily, F. "A Study of Female Teachers' Verbal Behavior and Peer-group Structure Among Classes of Fifth-grade Children." Unpublished Doctoral Dissertation, Kent State University, Kent, Ohio, 1970.

EDUCATION, U. S. A. Arlington, V.A.: National School Public Relations Association, September 4, 1978.

Flanders, N. *Analyzing Teacher Behavior.* Reading, MA: Addison Wesley, 1970.

Joyce, B. and Showers, B. *Student Achievement Through Staff Development.* New York: Longman, 1988.

Kohlberg, L. et al. *Assessing Moral Stages, A Manual.* Cambridge, M.A.: Harvard University Press, 1978.

Kohn, A. "Art for Art's Sake," *Psychology Today.* Vol. 21, No. 9. September, 1987.

Lepper, M. and Green, D. (Eds.) *The Hidden Cost of Rewards: New Perspectives on the Psychology of Human Motivation.* New York: Erlbaum, 1978.

Lowery, L. and Marshall, H. *Learning About Instruction: Teacher-initiated Statements and Questions.* Berkeley, CA: University of California, 1980.

Rowe, M. B. "Wait Time and Rewards as Instructional Variables: Their Influence on Language, Logic and Fate Control," *Journal of Research in Science Teaching.* Vol. 11, 81-94, 1974.

Soar, R. "Pupil Teacher Interaction," in *A New Look at Progressive Education: Yearbook of the Association for Supervision and Curriculum Development.* J. Squire Ed. Alexandria, V.A.: Association for Supervision and Curriculum Development, 1972.

Wallen, N. W. and Woodke, J. H. *Relationships between Teacher Characteristics and Student Behavior, Part I.* Salt Lake City: Department of Educational Psychology, University of Utah, 1963.

Thinking Skills: Neither An Add-On Nor A Quick Fix

The educational reform movement of the 80s is stressing the development of students' thinking abilities in preparing them for the information age of the future. In the tradition of past reform movements, many educators were quick to jump on bandwagons making politically expedient and financially parsimonious decisions. Recent experiences with many school districts' efforts to install *thinking* as a goal of education, however, have turned my head around.

Happily, what is being witnessed is a dedication to incorporate the *education of the intellect* neither as an add-on nor a quick fix. Rather, cognitive curriculum is serving as the basis for reconsideration of our theoretical foundations, a realistic view of what is basic for all learners, and a thoughtful dedication to long-range planning and development. What follows are some joyful observations of these new directions and an invitation to compare them with your own progress.

What's Basic

Recent research, while not yet sufficient to confirm, tends to indicate that when thinking skills become an integral part of the curriculum and instructional practice, test scores in academic areas increase (Whimbey 1985). It seems that the ability to perform certain cognitive processes is basic to success in school subjects. Hierarchical thinking, for example, when taught prior to or along with the skill of outlining produces better results than if taught without that cognitive prerequisite. When reading is taught as a strategy of thinking, students seem to increase their comprehension (Andre 1979). When teachers take the time to teach comparative behavior, for example, students are better able to contrast the differing points of view of the North and the South during the Civil War using a consistent set of attributes (Beyer 1985).

As a result, many educators are forming a new understanding of what is a basic skill. We are realizing that there is a prerequisite to the "basics"—the ability to think.

Thinking Is For All Students

For many years we thought that thinking skills programs were intended to challenge the intellectually gifted. Indeed, some thought that any child whose I.Q. fell below a certain static score was forever doomed to remedial or compensatory drill and practice.

Gaining wide acceptance, four fundamental and refreshing concepts underlie modern cognitive curriculum and instructional practices. They are: The Theory of Cognitive Modifiability (Feuerstein 1980), the Theory of Multiple Intelligences (Gardner 1983), the faith that Intelligence Can be Taught (Whimbey 1975), and Sternberg's thesis that traditional I.Q. scores have very little to do with success in dealing with the problems encountered in daily life (Hammer 1985 and McKean 1985).

These theoretical concepts equip us with the realization that *all* human beings are both retarded in certain problem-solving skills, while simultaneously being gifted in others (Link as quoted by Makler, 1980). They provide us the faith that *all* human beings can continue to develop their intelligent behavior throughout a lifetime. Indeed much research with hydrocephalic, Down's Syndrome,

senile, and brain-damaged persons demonstrates that over time and with proper intervention, they can continue to make amazing growth in problem-solving abilities. Until recently, we would have given them up as hopeless.

Furthermore, and perhaps most reassuring, we are demonstrating that increasing the effectiveness of instruction produces a corresponding increase in learning. Teachers *can* grow intelligence.

Language And Thought In Loco Parentis

We are increasingly aware of the close connection and interaction between language and thought processes. Vygotsky and Piaget taught us this long ago. Perhaps we never realized it so fully, however, until it was made apparent through recent sociological upheavals.

We know that most cognitive structures are built in children's minds within the first few years of life—long before they come to school—and that these schema are the result of (along with other nutritional, genetic, and environmental factors) interactions with significant adults in the child's environment.

With the transition of the traditional family in our culture, with increasing numbers of "latchkey kids," with an increasing number of children giving birth to children, and with a dramatic increase in passive television watching, there has been a corresponding decrease in the amount of verbal interaction between parents and children in the home. Indeed, some students come to school parentally deprived.

Correlations have been found between the complexity of language used in the home, the mental develop-ment of the child, and the family's affluence or educational level. Sternberg and Caruso (1985) report increasing complexity of language and questioning tendencies in families at higher socio-economic levels.

Realizing that thinking is basic, and that children's early language (and therefore cognitive) development may be lacking, we are witnessing a new direction for classroom instruction: *increasing verbal interaction.* Teaching and learning are invigorated with increased opportunities for dialogue: developing listening skills, cooperative learning, pair problem solving, thought-provoking inquiry discussions, dialogical reasoning, collaborative planning, and brainstorming. Teach-ers are finding renewed power as they stimulate students' thought processes by using challenging questions and probing. They search for increases in diversity and creativity of students' responses as they provide a safe, non-judgmental classroom environment in which students can risk verbalizing innovative ideas (Costa 1985).

Expanding Definitions: From Thinking Skills To Intelligent Behavior

As schools begin the process of infusing thinking skills into their curriculum and instructional practices, they often start with the task of defining what it means—just what are thinking skills? This search seems to begin with a rather narrow list of cognitive skills—classifying, inferring, categorizing, hypothesizing, etc. Soon, however, some perplexing questions arise: How are these skills applied in a wide variety of subject areas and problem-solving situations? How are they transferred from situations in which they were learned to life situations outside the school? Should creativity, social skills, and ethical/moral reasoning be included in the definition? Resolving these concerns seems to cause an expansion of the concept of thinking from narrow definitions and lists of discrete skills to a more generalized, all-encompassing set of descriptors of what human beings do when they behave intelligently (Glatthorn and Baron 1985 and Ennis 1985).

From research on what "good thinkers" do when they solve problems, the definition of thinking skills is being enlarged to include such generic behaviors as persistence, flexibility, striving for precision and accuracy, reducing impulsivity, considering others' points of view, supporting conclusions with evidence, risk-taking, metacognition, and empathy.

Pervasive—
Not An Add-On

Refocusing on this larger picture seems to encourage the acceptance and applicability of teaching thinking to a wider range of teachers' interests, subject matter, grade levels, and learning activities.

All teachers can agree that such cognitive skills as following directions, striving for precision, checking for accuracy, perseverance, listening to others' points of view, and creativity are basic to their discipline. *Organizational skills* are as basic to the auto shop as they are to the physics laboratory. *Planning ahead* is as much a requirement in the home economics curriculum as it is in written composition. *Being alert to cues* is a survival skill applicable in driver training and in preparation for marriage and family life.

As a result of this wider acceptance, thinking skills are *not* being viewed as mere additions to an already over-crowded, time-squeezed, cemeterial compendium of scopes and sequences. Rather, teachers are finding comfort, agreement, and rededication in some common goals—that process is as important as product; that thoughtful and reflective teaching (rather than coverage) is acceptable once again; and that students' *production* of knowledge is as important as their *reproduction* of knowledge.

Give It Time

Unlike many other educational innovations and experiments, educational planners are viewing the infusion of thinking skills as a three- to five-year process. They are realizing that such a change cannot be a quick fix. Rather, it requires altering instructional strategies, communicating with community and parents, reevaluating class schedules, reorganizing curriculum materials and evaluation techniques, and rededicating the basic value system and norms of entire faculties.

They are realizing that the process of change must be consistent with the product of that change. If teachers are expected to teach reflectiveness, rationality, and reason to students, then the processes of curriculum development and educational improvement must also involve reflective, rational, and reasoned decision making (Bellanca 1985).

Taking precious classroom time to teach thinking is gaining acceptance. We've known that the amount of time on task affects student learning. This relationship is as true for academic achievement as it is for acquiring thinking skills. When thinking becomes a goal of instruction, teachers and administrators place greater value on allocating classroom time for learning activities intended to stimulate, practice, and discuss cognitive processes.

Schools As Intellectually Stimulating Places

Perhaps it is a happy combination of applying school effectiveness research, improving the professionalism of education, and the emphasis on cognitive education. John Goodlad's (1983) generalized description of schools in our country as being intellectually depressing places is giving way to the stimulation of teachers' intellectual processes. It is hypothesized that teachers will not teach for thinking unless they are in an intellectually stimulating environment themselves.

As a result, teachers are feeling a greater sense of efficacy—gaining more control of and becoming involved in those school and district level decisions that affect them most. This trend is in sharp contrast to the recent view of the teacher's role as being accountable for implementing decisions being mandated from "above."

Teachers' thinking, decision making, and problem solving are being enhanced because they are viewing the act of teaching as a creative, experimental, problem-solving, decision-making process rather than a recipe to follow. (Indeed, teaching by the number is as equally creative as painting by the number.) Renewed interest is being exhibited in developing teachers' repertoire of teaching strategies (Joyce 1985) rather than in training a narrow range of instructional behaviors. Teachers are jointly planning lessons, teaching strategies and curriculum, and then opening their classroom doors, inviting their colleagues and supervisors to observe their interaction, to gain feedback about the thinking skills students display, and to search for ways of enhancing cognition.

It is with renewed excitement, therefore, that participation in the educational profession is intellectually growth-producing for *all* its constituents (Sprinthall and Theis-Sprinthall 1983).

Evaluation— A Paradigm Shift

Usually when we think of gathering evidence of pupil achievement, we think of tests—norm-referenced, paper-and-pencil, multiple-choice. Efforts by several states (California, Vermont, Pennsylvania, New Jersey, and Connecticut) are revising test items to include critical thinking in their assessment programs (Kneedler 1985 and Baron and Kallick 1985).

With the need to assess growth in thinking skills, we are finding, however, that some of our traditional assessment techniques are inadequate. One reason is that performance on a test is overt; but thinking is a covert process and thus not directly observable and measurable in our traditional, behavioristic ways (Winocur 1985).

Another reason is that tests usually seek to determine how many answers a student knows. Rather, we are witnessing a refocus of assessment practices on how the student behaves when the answer is *not* known—how they behave in every-day, problem-solving situations. Thus the focus on learning OF objectives is being replaced by learning FROM objectives (Andre 1979).

We are finding renewed interest in longitudinal growth studies such as development of study teams, and the collection of anecdotal records and portfolios of students' work which may reflect cognitive development over time. Teachers are becoming alert to the clues, found in everyday classroom problem solving, which indicate growth in intelligent behaviors (Baron and Kallick 1985).

Not Just Educators— Parents And Industry, Too

Free enterprise, entrepreneurship, innovation, problem solving, creativity—industrial leaders are telling educators about their needs for the twenty-first century. The information age is well upon us. The work force of the future needs skills in collaborative problem solving, being alert to problems as they arise, handling massive amounts of information, and innovative ways to deliver a product more quickly, efficiently, and economically (Education Commission of the States 1982).

By some estimates it is predicted that workers of the future will be changing jobs five to six times during their careers. Flexibility, continuing to learn how to learn, and dealing with ambiguity and change seem to be the paramount survival skills of the future.

Because of this need, industry is realizing education as the lifeblood of their future. New alliances and partnerships are being formed between schools, communities, and businesses in an effort to learn from each other about the need for and development of intelligent and creative behavior (Dageforde 1985).

Modeling

With the understanding that imitation is the most basic form of learning, teachers, parents, and administrators are realizing the importance of their display of desirable intelligent behaviors in the presence of children. Thus, in day-to-day events and when problems arise in schools, classrooms, and homes, students must see adults employing the same types of behaviors that the new curriculum demands.

Without this consistency, there is likely to be a credibility gap. As Emerson is often quoted, "What you do speaks so loudly they can't hear what you say."

From the cumulative effects of these efforts we are finding that all the members of the educational enterprise—teachers, administrators, trustees, parents, and students are profiting. All are becoming more rational, thoughtful, and creative in the process. Indeed, thinking about thinking is producing more thinking.

References

Andre, T. "Does Answering Higher-level Questions While Reading Facilitate Productive Learning?" *Review of Educational Research* 49, no. 2 (Spring 1979): 280-318.

Baron, J. and Kallick, B. "What are We Looking For and How Can We Find It?" In *Developing Minds: A Resource Book For Teaching Thinking.* Ed. A. Costa. Alexandria, VA: Association of Supervision and Curriculum Development, 1985.

Bellanca, J. "A Call for Staff Development." In *Developing Minds: A Resource Book For Teaching Thinking.* Ed. A. Costa. Alexandria, VA: Association for Supervision and Curriculum Development, 1985.

Beyer, B. "Critical Thinking: What is It?" *Social Education* 40 (April, 1985): 271-76.

Costa, A. "Teacher Behaviors That Enhance Thinking." In *Developing Minds: A Resource Book For Teaching Thinking.* Ed. A. Costa. Alexandria, VA: Association for Supervision and Curriculum Development, 1985.

Dageforde, L. "Partnerships in Industry and Education." Presentation at the Project IMPACT Leadership Training, Orange County Superintendent of Schools Office, Costa Mesa, California, August 27, 1985.

Education Commission of the States. Denver, 1982.

Ennis, R. "Critical Thinking: A Definition." In *Developing Minds: A Resource Book For Teaching Thinking..* Ed. A. Costa. Alexandria, VA: Association for Supervision and Curriculum Development, 1985.

Feuerstein, R. *Instrumental Enrichment.* Baltimore: University Park Press, 1980.

Gardner, H. *Frames of Mind: The Theory of Multiple Intelligences.* New York: Basic Books, 1983.

Glatthorn, A. and Baron, J. "The Good Thinker." In *Developing Minds: A Resource Book For Teaching Thinking.* Ed. A. Costa. Alexandria, VA: Association for Supervision and Curriculum Development, 1985.

Goodlad, J. *A Place Called School: Prospects For The Future.* New York: McGraw-Hill, 1983.

Hammer, S. "Stalking Intelligence." *Science Digest* 93 (June 6, 1985): 30-38.

Joyce, B. "Models for Teaching Thinking." *Educational Leadership* 42, no. 8 (May 1985): 4-9.

Kneedler, P. "California Assesses Critical Thinking." In *Developing Minds: A Resource Book For Teaching Thinking.* Ed. A. Costa. Alexandria, VA: Association for Supervision and Curriculum Development, 1985.

Makler, S. "Instrumental Enrichment: A Conversation with Francis Link." *Educational Leadership.* (April, 1980).

McKean, K. "The Assault on IQ." *Discover* 6, no. 10 (October 1985): 25-41.

Sprinthall, N. and Theis-Sprinthall, L. "The Teacher as an Adult Learner: A Cognitive Developmental View." In *Staff Development:* Ed. G. Griffin. 82nd Yearbook of the National Society for the Study of Education. Chicago: University of Chicago Press, 1983.

Sternberg, R. and Caruso, D. "Practical Modes of Knowing." In *Learning And Teaching The Ways Of Knowing.* Ed. E. Eisner. Eighty-Fourth Yearbook of the National Society for the Study of Education, Part II. Chicago: University of Chicago Press, 1985.

Whimbey, A. "The Consequences of Teaching Thinking." In *Developing Minds: A Resource Book For Teaching Thinking.* Ed. A. Costa. Alexandria, VA: Association for Supervision and Curriculum Development, 1985.

Whimbey, A. and Whimbey, L. *Intelligence Can Be Taught.* New York: Bantam Books, 1976.

Winocur, S. L. "Developing Lesson Plans with Cognitive Objectives." In *Developing Minds: A Resource Book For Teaching Thinking.* Ed. A. Costa. Alexandria, VA: Association for Supervision and Curriculum Development, 1985.

———— ✌ ————

Teaching A Thinking Skill Or Strategy Directly

Mrs. Englander, the kindergarten teacher, stood erect before the children. Her arms were folded tightly across her chest; her lips were tightened and curled down at the ends. Below a wrinkled forehead and depressed eyebrows two squinting dark eyes stared piercingly at the children.

"What's wrong?" one child inquired. "Are you mad at us?" "Don't you feel well?" "Is there something wrong?" "Are you angry?" "Did you get up on the wrong side of the bed?" they asked.

"Today we're going to learn what an inference is," began Mrs. Englander.

Does the curriculum of your school include learning how to divide? Does it include learning how to *infer?* Does it include learning how to multiply? Does it include learning how to *compare?* To *generalize?* To *prioritize?*

If learning to think is to become a reality in education, then it is believed that classroom time should be devoted to teaching thinking skills directly—

that teaching the processes of thinking should become the content of instruction. Like any skill, it needs to be taught explicitly, its steps should be analyzed, it should be practiced across a varied range of situations, and applied to conditions beyond the context in which it was learned.

We often find a science textbook, for example, which asks students to make a *conclusion* based upon data observed during an experiment. We assume students know how to draw conclusions, yet we seldom teach students that skill. We may hear ourselves or other teachers ask questions that presuppose students' knowing how to perform certain thinking skills: "Who can *summarize* some of the things we've learned about the nomads of the desert?" "Let's *analyze* this problem." "How does Jamie's report *compare* with Shannon's?"

While we may assume that students know how to perform the thinking skills implied in the subject matter and the instructional interactions being used in the classroom, we often find they have never learned what it means to perform these basic thinking skills. As a result, students are often dismayed, confused, and handicapped when asked to perform them.

When thinking skills are taught directly, academic achievement seems to increase (de Bono 1984 and Whimbey 1985). Advocates (such as Barry Beyer 1985) of the direct teaching of thinking skills report that performance on tests increases when time is taken to teach thinking. Furthermore, it signals the students to what is important. When time is devoted to lessons on thinking, students get the message that thinking is an important learning.

When teaching a thinking skill directly, the content becomes the vehicle for thinking. For example, students can learn the process of *classifying* using this week's spelling list. We can teach *comparison* during a handwriting lesson in which students learn how to form a "d" and a "b". We can teach students to distinguish *fact* and *opinion* during current events in the social studies class. We want students to master the content, *and* we can seize opportunities from the academic subject students are learning to teach a thinking skill directly.

Thinking skills are best taught when:

1) Students are developmentally ready for that form of thinking. It does little good, for example, to teach students to classify using multiple classification systems and several sources of data simultaneously in kindergarten or first grade. (Larry Lowery's article (1985), "The Biological Basis for Thinking", offers insight as to when students are developmentally ready for certain thinking skills.)

2) The thinking skill is relevant to and will be used successfully and repeatedly in immediate and future learnings. Teaching thinking skills in isolation is of little value. While they may be a joyous learning experience, there will be greater transfer if the students see how it will help them *and* if there will be several occasions in the near future to revisit, practice, and apply that skill.

Following is a description of:

1) a lesson planning strategy for teaching a thinking skill directly;

2) two suggested lessons intended to illustrate that lesson design; and

3) ways you may search for other opportunities to teach a thinking skill directly.

A Lesson Planning Strategy For Teaching A Thinking Skill

This lesson design is based upon the model of thinking presented in Costa (1985). It is presented here again for review.

The thinking skill to be learned may be:

- Defined by the teacher or the students

- Recalled if students have previous experience with it

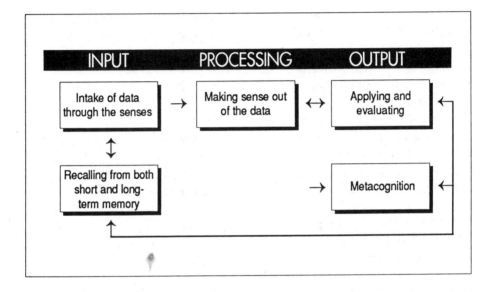

Using this model as a guide, what follows is a generic lesson plan for teaching a thinking skill directly. It is based upon four major steps:

I. Input

During this stage the teacher calls attention to the specific thinking skill or strategy as the focus of the lesson. It will be explained to be the objective of the lesson, why it is an important skill to learn, when it will be used, etc.

- Modeled by the teacher using familiar content

- Observed as the teacher or student or skilled person performs it

- Discussed by the observers

Furthermore, vocabulary related to this skill should be built— antonyms, synonyms, similar words or processes, and related words should be introduced.

II. Process

During this phase the students should become conscious of and discuss what goes on in their head when this thinking skill is being performed. What are the steps in the process?

The class may be organized in small groups to actually *experience* the skill. A task, using familiar content should be provided in which the performance of the skill is required. They should be asked to think about their own thinking while they are performing the task.

A *thinking observer* could be appointed to record what the group members did while they were completing the task.

When the group has completed the task, ask them to *analyze* the metacognitive components. With the help of the observer, discuss what went on inside their head as they were completing the task.

The metacognitive steps are *sequenced*: what was the first thing they did, what came next, then what, etc.

III. Output

During this phase, the skill should be performed again but should be applied to a new setting. The content should be changed but the skill used again beyond the context in which it was learned. This time it could be performed individually.

The teacher could ask the students to be conscious of their own metacognitive processes while they are completing the task. Their earlier descriptions of what they did during the *process* phase should be compared and refined.

The skill should be bridged or *transferred* to other uses in school subjects, life, or careers. Students may be asked how they would use this skill in other subject areas; in other classes; at home, play, or with friends. They could describe professions or careers in which workers use this skill daily.

IV. Review

Soon after the skill was taught and periodically throughout the year, the skill needs to be reviewed when it is required in a learning task. As other opportunities arise in future lessons, a brief review may be required.

The intent of teaching thinking skills directly is to cause students to use them automatically—spontaneously, without the teacher's intervention. Teachers will want to be on the lookout for instances in which students voluntarily perform the skills they were taught previously.

Sample Lesson For Teaching A Thinking Skill Directly
THINKING SKILL: Classification/Categorization
Input:

Focus: Tell the students that the purpose of the lesson is to learn what it means to categorize and to classify and why it is necessary to learn such skills.

Vocabulary: classify, attribute, group, sort, categorize, characteristic, compare, contrast.

Ask them to discuss, define, and distinguish the meanings of the words: *classify, categorize, group,* and *sort.*

Classifying means to arrange objects in groups based upon similarities *and* to label those groups using a name that carries the significant attributes of the members of that group. *Citrus,* for example is a label given to a class of fruit. No other fruits have the same attributes of citrus other than those members of that class.

Categorizing means that the label is given and it is your responsibility to list members of that group. When I say "root vegetables" for example, what can you list under that label: carrots, beets, radishes, etc.

Sorting means to take from a collection of random objects and to put those items together that have like characteristics. Sorting laundry according to permanent press, colored, whites, etc.

Grouping means to assemble those items based upon some common characteristics or attribute.

Demonstrate classifying and categorizing by giving a list of familiar fruits (for example):

grapefruit	lemon	peach
apricot	plum	pear
nectarine	apple	lime
cherry	orange	tangerine

Ask them to put all those that are alike together and to give that group a label:

Citrus	*Stonefruit*	*Core (Pom)*
grapefruit	apricot	pear
orange	plum	apple
lemon	peach	
lime	cherry	
nectarine		

Ask them to then *Categorize*: Give them the labels:

Root Vegetables   Leafy Vegetables

Invite them to generate examples of items in each category.

Process: Present a list of words. (It could be the week's spelling list or a list of vocabulary words from the science or social studies textbook). Ask students to work in small groups to *classify* the words and to think about what goes on in their heads when they classify.

segment	finger	corner	angle
shoulder	line	square	surface
machine	magnet	reel	
circle	strut	wheel	
plane	stomach	mouth	

There is not one way to correctly classify this list. What is important is that students experience the process of classification and that they justify why they chose the groups and labels as they did. Following is only one way:

Mechanical Words	*Human Body*	*Geometric Terms*
machine	shoulder	segment
plane	finger	circle
reel	mouth	plane
strut	stomach	line
magnet		square
wheel		angle
		surface
		corner

Ask the students and the *Thinking Process Observer* to share what they did when they classified (metacognition). Record their contributions on an overhead, a chart or the board randomly as they are given. They may be something like this:

When We Classify We:

Scan the list.
Look for similarities between the words.
Try a label to see if there are other words that might fit.
Define the words.
Pick a label, then fit the other words into that label.
Decide what to do with words that fit more than one category (plane).
Decide what to do with words that are "left over."
Sub-classify words within categories.
Expand the label to fit other words in the list.
Check to see that all words are accounted for.
Call on previous knowledge of what words mean.
Decide a purpose for classifying words.

Next ask the students to reflect on the sequence of steps. What did they do first, second, third, etc. Refine the list accordingly.

Output: Now invite the students to apply what they have learned about classifying to a new situation.

Ask your students for some help in straightening up your desk drawers (or cupboards, or storage closets). Divide the class into three or four groups or teams. Assign each team a drawer, a cupboard, or a closet. Ask them to take all the objects out and classify them. Again appoint a *Thinking Process Observer* to collect data about the group's metacognitive steps in completing the task.

When complete, ask the groups to discuss their classifications and what they did in the process of classifying. Return to the list of metacognitive operations generated in the processing phase. Refine the list as needed.

Ask students to bridge to other subject areas. When else do

they need to classify? How would it help them if they kept the steps of classification in mind as they performed a learning task?

Ask students to bridge to other times outside of school when they need to classify (allocating allowance, going to the supermarket, using the library, etc.).

Invite students to think about professions and careers in which classification is essential (postal workers, librarians, sales-people, zookeepers, etc.).

Ask students to identify examples of classification systems they use (zip codes, Dewey decimal system, area codes, etc.).

Review: As other learning experiences requiring classification and categorization abilities are encountered in the curriculum, have students recall what it means to classify. Review what they must keep in mind during the learning. Encourage students to use the terminology correctly, distinguishing precise meanings between words: classification, categorization, sorting, grouping, etc.

For example: in a science lesson, students are asked to categorize objects into solids, liquids, and gasses. Before they begin, review with them definitions, what the steps are in the process.

Thinking Strategy: Following Directions (adapted from Feuerstein, 1980)

Input: Tell the students about an experience you've had in which you've had to follow somebody else's instructions: asking for directions while driving (you can't miss it), assembling an unassembled machine or toy, etc. Describe the difficulties you had because of the lack of clarity of directions. Invite students to share similar events. Discuss with them why it is important to give and receive clear instructions.

Vocabulary:

instruction	command	direction	explicit
encode	implied	description	implicit
order	rule	plan	directive

Invite students to define and distinguish between these words.

Explain that directions come in many forms. (A separate lesson could easily be built around each of these definitions.)

1. Commands: "Shut the door." "Sit down." "Stop running." Very little thought is needed to obey such commands. You just do it. Invite students to generate more examples of commands.

2. Some directions are given indirectly and require more thought. To follow them requires the analysis of implicit instructions. In a recipe, "simmer at a low temperature" implies that you must turn on the burner of the stove, place the food to be cooked in a pan, etc. Invite students to generate more examples from their experience.

3. Some directions require you to combine the instructions with a description about which some judgment must be made: "Bake the muffins at 400 degrees or until *golden brown*." "Fry until *tender*, turning *occasionally*." They require you to judge for yourself when it is done and how often it should be turned. Invite students to generate more examples from their experience.

4. Some instructions require the application of a rule, law, or definition: "Divide 1/2 by 1/5" implies the inversion of one fraction. "How much is one half of two plus three," implies the performance of a sequence of arithmetical operations.

5. Some instructions are not verbal; rather they are symbolic. Sometimes the directions which accompany machinery or tools simply say "Assemble as shown," and we must interpret what they mean. Sometimes symbols in buildings give us a command which we must interpret for ourselves.

Have students generate other examples.

Process: Dictate to the class a somewhat complicated set of instructions. Ask them to be conscious of what goes on inside their heads while instructions are followed. For example:

Have students draw a two-inch frame on a piece of scratch paper.

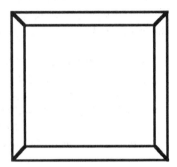

Recite to them the following instructions: *"In the center of your frame draw a circle, a square, and a triangle. The other two figures should be inside the circle. Only the triangle should be empty."*

Have them draw the figure and keep track of their metacognitive processes.

Next invite them to share what went on inside their heads when following a direction.

Record their ideas on the board, overhead, or chart:

When We Follow Instructions We:

1. Listen to, read, or study carefully all the directions. Gather all the data first.
2. Don't start before we make sure you know what to do.
3. Make a mental picture inside our heads of what the completed product will look like if completed correctly.
4. Do it.
5. Check it. Compare our product with the image held inside our heads or with another person.

Output: Give other complicated directions for students to follow. They may be found in textbooks, recipe books, technical manuals, repair kits, income tax forms, application blanks, etc.

As they become aware of following directions, have them refine their list of metacognitive functions.

Invite them to think of situations at home, in the community, in school when following directions is essential. (Taking tests, applying for a job, paying bills, driving, etc.)

Invite them to interview parents and relatives about when and how they need to give and follow instruction.

Invite them to generate categories of jobs in which workers must give and follow instructions (architects, contractors, mechanics, programmers, travel agents, etc.).

Review: As assignments are made and directions for tests and homework is given, have students review the metacognitive steps in following directions.

As you give instructions, be sure:

• they are given in several modalities to maximize input.
• students discuss, or you model, or they model, or they say in their own words what those instructions mean (this helps to make a mental picture of the final product).
• to give them adequate time to complete while you monitor their progress.
• to have them check their paper with other students or with parents before they turn it in to you.

Ways Teachers Can Add To Their Teaching Of Thinking Skills Directly

After trying the above lesson design format, you may wish to add to your list and develop lesson plans around other discrete skills and strategies. It is fairly easy to do if you will be conscious of your own thinking processes.

Keep track of what you do when you think critically or creatively. Be aware of the metacognitive components in the process. Next time you have a problem to solve, a special lesson to plan, or a particularly challenging situation which "taxes" your mind, keep track of the thinking processes. How do you solve the problem—step by step.

After you consciously track your thinking skills in this way, you can then translate them into learning opportunities for students. For example, following is a numerical progression. Be conscious of what you do when you predict what the next number/letter combination will be:

20C 18E 16G 14I ___ ___

References

Bellanca, J. and Fogarty, R. *Mental Menus: 24 Explicit Thinking Skills.* Palatine, IL: IRI/Skylight Publishing, 1986.

Beyer, B. "Practical strategies for the direct teaching of thinking skills." In A. Costa (Ed.), *Developing Minds: A Resource Book For Teaching Thinking.* Alexandria VA: Association for Supervision and Curriculum Development, 1985.

Costa, A. "Towards a Model of Human Intellectual Functioning." In A. Costa (Ed.), *Developing Minds: A Resource Book For Teaching Thinking.* Alexandria VA: Association for Supervision and Curriculum Development, 1985.

de Bono, E. "Critical Thinking is Not Enough." *Educational Leadership,* September, 42(1), 16-18, 1984.

Feuerstein, R. *Instrumental Enrichment.* Baltimore: University Park Press, 1980.

Lowery, L. "The Biological Basis for Thinking." In A. Costa (Ed.), *Developing Minds: A Resource Book For Teaching Thinking.* Alexandria VA: Association for Supervision and Curriculum Development, 1985.

Whimbey, A. "Test Results from Teaching Thinking." In A. Costa (Ed.), *Developing Minds: A Resource Book For Teaching Thinking.* Alexandria VA: Association for Supervision and Curriculum Development, 1985.

Mediating The Metacognitive

Try to solve this problem in your head: How much is one half of two plus two?

Did you hear yourself talking to yourself? Did you find yourself having to decide if you should take one half of the first two (which would give the answer, three) or if you should sum the two's first (which would give the answer, two)?

If you caught yourself having an "inner" dialogue inside your brain, and if you had to stop to evaluate your own decision-making/problem-solving processes, you were experiencing *metacognition.*

Occurring in the neocortex and therefore thought by some neurologists to be uniquely human, metacognition is our ability to know what we know and what we don't know. It is our ability to plan a strategy for producing what information is needed, to be conscious of our own steps and strategies during the act of problem solving, and to reflect on and evaluate the productiveness of our own thinking. While "inner language," thought to be a prerequisite, begins in most children around age five, metacognition is a key attribute of formal thought flowering about age eleven. Interestingly, not all humans achieve the level of formal operations (Chiabetta 1976). And as Alexander Luria, the Russian psychologist found, not all adults metacogitate (Whimbey 1976).

We often find students following instructions or performing tasks without wondering why they are doing what they are doing. They seldom question themselves about their own learning strategies or evaluate the efficiency of their own performance. Some children virtually have no idea of what they should do when they confront a problem and are often unable to explain their strategies of decision making (Sternberg and Wagner 1982). There is much evidence, however, to demonstrate that those who perform well on complex cognitive tasks, who are flexible and persevere in problem solving, who consciously apply their intellectual skills, are those who possess well-developed metacognitive abilities (Bloom and Broder 1950; Brown 1978; and Whimbey 1980). They are those who "manage" their intellectual resources well: 1) their basic perceptual-motor skills; 2) their language, beliefs, knowledge of content, and memory processes; and 3) their purposeful and voluntary strategies intended to achieve a desired outcome (Aspen Institute 1982).

If we wish to install intelligent behavior as a significant outcome of education, then instructional strategies, purposefully intended to develop children's metacognitive abilities, must be infused into our teaching methods, staff development, and supervisory processes (Costa 1981). Interestingly, *direct* instruction in metacognition may *not* be beneficial. When strategies of problem solving are imposed by the teacher rather than generated by the students themselves, their performance may become impaired. Conversely, when students experience the need for problem-solving strategies, induce their own, discuss, and practice them to the degree that they become spontaneous and unconscious, their metacognition seems to improve (Sternberg and Wagner 1982). The trick, therefore, is to teach metacognitive skills without creating an even greater burden on their ability to attend to the task.

Probably the major components of metacognition are developing a plan of action, maintaining that plan in mind over a period of time, then reflecting back on and evaluating the plan upon its completion. Planning a strategy before embarking on a course of action assists us in keeping track of the steps in the sequence of planned behavior at the conscious awareness level for the duration of the activity. It facilitates making temporal and comparative judgments, assessing the readiness for more or different activities, and monitoring our interpretations, perceptions, decisions, and behaviors. An example of this would be what superior teachers do daily: developing a teaching strategy for a lesson, keeping that strategy in mind throughout the instruction, then reflecting back upon the strategy to evaluate its effectiveness in producing the desired student outcomes.

Rigney (1980) identified the following self-monitoring skills as necessary for successful performance on intellectual tasks:

- keeping one's place in a long sequence of operations;

- knowing that a subgoal has been obtained; and

- detecting errors and recovering from those errors either by making a quick fix or by retreating to the last known correct operation.

Such monitoring involves both "looking ahead" and "looking back." Looking ahead includes:

- learning the structure of a sequence of operations and identifying areas where errors are likely;

- choosing a strategy that will reduce the possibility of error and will provide easy recovery; and

- identifying the kinds of feedback that will be available at various points, and evaluating the usefulness of that feedback.

Looking back includes:

- detecting errors previously made;

- keeping a history of what has been done to the present and thereby what should come next; and

- assessing the reasonableness of the present immediate outcome of task performance.

A simple example of this might be drawn from a reading task. It is a common experience while reading a passage to have our mind "wander" from the pages. We "see" the words but no meaning is being produced. Suddenly we realize that we are not concentrating and that we've lost contact with the meaning of the text. We "recover" by returning to the passage to find our place, matching it with the last thought we can remember, and, once having found it, reading

on with connectedness. This inner awareness and the strategy of recovery are components of metacognition.

Strategies For Enhancing Metacognition*

Following are a dozen suggestions that teachers of any grade level can use to enhance metacognition. Whether teaching vocational education, physical education, algebra, or reading skills, teachers can promote metacognition by using these and similar instructional techniques.

1. Strategy Planning

Prior to any learning activity, teachers will want to take time to develop and discuss strategies and steps for attacking problems, rules to remember, and directions to be followed. Time constraints, purposes, and ground rules under which students must operate should be developed and "interiorized." Thus, students can better keep these in mind during and evaluate their performance after the experience.

During the activity, teachers can invite students to share their progress, thought processes, and perceptions of

---

* For several of these techniques I am deeply indebted to Fred Newton, Multnomah County (Oregon) Superintendent of Schools Office; Juanita Sagan, a therapist in Oakland, California; and Ron Brandt of ASCD.

their own behavior. Asking students to indicate where they are in their strategy, to describe the "trail" of thinking up to that point, and what alternative pathways they intend to pursue next in the solution of their problem, helps them become aware of their own behavior. (It also provides the teacher with a diagnostic "cognitive map" of the student's thinking which can be used to give more individualized assistance.)

Then, *after* the learning activity is completed, teachers can invite students to evaluate how well those rules were obeyed, how productive were the strategies, whether the instructions were followed correctly, and what would be some alternative, more efficient strategies to be used in the future.

I know a kindergarten teacher who begins and ends each day with a class meeting. During these times, children make plans for the day. They decide upon what learning tasks to accomplish and how to accomplish them. They allocate classroom space, assign roles, and develop criteria for appropriate conduct. Throughout the day the teacher calls attention to the plans and ground rules made that morning and invites students to compare what they are doing with what was agreed. Then, before dismissal, another class meeting is held to reflect on, evaluate, and plan further strategies and criteria.

2. Question Generating

Regardless of the subject area, it is useful for students to pose study questions for themselves prior to and during their reading of textual material. This self-generation of questions facilitates comprehension. It encourages the student to pause frequently and perform a "self-check" for understanding, to determine whether or not comprehension has occurred. Comprehension can be said to have occurred if, for example, they know the main characters or events; they are grasping the concept; it "makes sense"; they can relate it to what they already know; they can give other examples or instances; they can use the main idea to explain other ideas; or they can use the information in the passage to predict what may come next. They then must decide what strategic action should be taken to remove obstacles that thereby increase comprehension. This helps students become more self-aware and to take conscious control of their own studying (Sanacore 1984).

3. Conscious Choosing

Teachers can promote metacognition by helping students explore the consequences of their choices and decisions prior to and during the act of deciding. Students will then be able to perceive causal relationships between their choice, their actions, and the results they achieved. Providing nonjudgmental feedback about the effects of their behaviors and decisions on others and on their environment helps students become aware of their own behaviors. For example, a teacher's statement, "I want you to know that the noise you're making with your pencil is disturbing me," will better contribute to metacognitive development than the command, "John, stop tapping your pencil!"

4. Differentiated Evaluating

Teachers can enhance metacognition by causing students to reflect upon and categorize their actions according to two or more sets of evaluative criteria. Examples would be, inviting students to distinguish between what was done that day that helped and hindered; what they liked and didn't like; or what were pluses and minuses of the activity. Thus, students must keep the criteria in mind, apply them to multiple classification systems, and justify their reasons accordingly.

5. Taking Credit

Teachers may cause students to identify what they have done well and invite them to seek feedback from their peers. The teacher might ask, "What have you done that you're proud of?" "How would you like to be recognized for doing that?" (name on the board, hug, pat on the back, handshake, applause from the group, etc.). Thus students will become more conscious of their own behavior and apply a set of internal criteria for that behavior which they consider "good."

6. Outlawing "I can't"

Teachers can inform students that their excuses of "I can't," "I don't know how to," or "I'm too slow to" are unacceptable behaviors in the classroom. Rather, having students identify what information is required, what materials are needed, or what skills are lacking in their ability to perform the desired behavior is an alternative and acceptable response. This helps students identify the boundaries between what they know and what they need to know. It develops a persevering attitude and enhances the student's ability to create strategies that will produce needed data.

7. Paraphrasing or Reflecting Back Student Ideas

Paraphrasing, building upon, extending, and using student ideas can make students conscious of their own thinking. Some examples might be, "What you're telling me is. . .," or "What I hear in your plan are the following steps. . .," or "Let's work with Peter's strategy for a moment."

Inviting students to restate, translate, compare, and paraphrase each other's ideas causes them to become not only better listeners of other's thinking, but better listeners to their own thinking as well.

8. Labeling Student Behaviors

When the teacher places labels on students' cognitive processes, it can make them conscious of their own actions: "What I see you doing is making out a plan of action for. . ."; "What you are doing is called an experiment."; or "You're being very helpful to Mark by sharing your paints. That's an example of cooperation."

9. Clarifying Student Terminology

Students often use "hollow," vague, and nonspecific terminology. For example, in making value judgments students might be heard saying, "It's not fair. . ."; "He's too strict"; or "It's no good." Teachers need to get in the habit of clarifying these values. "What's *too* strict?" "What would be more fair?"

We sometimes hear students using nominalizations. "They're mean to me." (Who are they?) "We had to do that." (Who is we?) "Everybody has one." (Who is "everybody?") Thus, clarifying causes students to operationally define their terminology and to examine the premise on which their thinking is based. It is desirable that, as a result of such clarifying, students would become more specific and qualifying in their terminology.

For older children, above age eleven or so, it appears helpful to invite them to clarify their problem-solving processes. Causing them to describe their thinking while they are thinking seems to beget more thinking. Some examples might be, inviting students to talk aloud as they are solving a problem; discussing what is going on in their heads, for example, when they confront an unfamiliar word while reading; or what steps they are going through in deciding whether to buy some article at the store. After solving a problem, the teacher can invite a clarification of the processes used. "Sarah, you figured out that the answer was 44; Shawn says the answer is 33. Let's hear how you came up with 44; retrace your steps for us." Thus clarifying helps students to reexamine their own problem-solving processes, to identify their own errors and to self-correct. The teacher might ask a question such as, "How much is three plus four?" The student may reply, "12." Rather than merely correcting the student, the teacher may choose to clarify: "Gina, how did you arrive at that answer?" "Well, I multiplied four and three and got. . . oh, I see, I multiplied instead of added."

10. Role Playing and Simulations

Having students assume the roles of other persons causes them to consciously maintain in their head the attributes and characteristics of that person. Dramatization serves as an hypothesis or prediction of how that person would react in a certain situation. This also contributes to the reduction of ego-centered perceptions.

11. *Journal Keeping*

Writing and illustrating a personal log or a diary throughout an experience over a period of time causes the student to synthesize thoughts and actions and to translate them into symbolic form. The record also provides an opportunity to revisit initial perceptions, to compare the changes in those perceptions with the addition of more data, to chart the processes of strategic thinking and decision making, to identify the blind alleys and pathways taken, and to recall the successes and the "tragedies" of experimentation (a variation on writing journals would be making video and/or audio tape recordings of actions and performances over time).

12. *Modeling*

Of all the instructional techniques suggested, the one with the probability of greatest influence on students is that of teacher modeling. Since students learn best by imitating the significant adults around them, the teacher who publicly demonstrates metacognition will probably produce students who metacogitate. Some indicators of teacher's public metacognitive behavior might be:

- sharing their planning by describing their goals and objectives and giving reasons for their actions;

- making human errors but then being seen to recover from those errors by getting "back on track";

- admitting they do not know an answer but designing ways to produce an answer;

- seeking feedback and evaluation of their actions from others;

- having a clearly stated value system and making decisions consistent with that value system;

- being able to self-disclose by using adjectives that describe their own strengths and weaknesses; and

- demonstrating understanding and empathy by listening to and accurately describing the ideas and feelings of others.

Evaluating Growth In Metacognitive Abilities

We can determine if students are becoming more aware of their own thinking as they are able to describe what goes on in their head when they are thinking. When asked, they can list the steps and tell where they are in the sequence of a problem-solving strategy. They can trace the pathways and dead ends they took on the road to a problem solution. They can describe what data are lacking and their plans for producing those data.

We should see students persevering more when the solution to a problem is not immediately apparent. This means that they have systematic methods of analyzing a problem, knowing ways to begin, knowing what steps must be performed and when they are accurate or are in error. We should see students taking more pride in their efforts, becoming self-correcting, striving for craftsmanship and accuracy in their products, and becoming more autonomous in their problem-solving abilities.

Teaching for thinking is becoming the great educational emphasis for the 80s. Metacognition is an attribute of the "educated intellect." It must be included if thinking is to become a durable reality for the 90s and beyond.

References

Aspen Systems *Topics in Learning and Learning Disabilities.* Gaithersburg, MD: Aspen Systems Corp. Vol 2. No. 1. April, 1982.

Bloom, B. S. and Broder, L. J. *Problem-Solving Processes of College Students.* Chicago, IL: University of Chicago Press, 1950.

Brown, A. L. "Knowing When, Where, and How to Remember: A Problem of Metacognition." In Glaser (Ed.), *Advances in Instructional Psychology.* Hillsdale, NJ: Erlbaum, 1978.

Chiabetta, E. L. A. "Review of Piagetian Studies Relevant to Science Instruction at the Secondary and College Level." *Science Education,* 60, 253-261, 1976.

Costa, A. L. "Teaching for Intelligent Behavior." *Educational Leadership,* October, 39(1), 1981.

Rigney, J. W. "Cognitive Learning Strategies and Qualities in Information Processing." In R. Snow, P. Federico, and W. Montague (Eds.), *Aptitudes, Learning, and Instruction,* Volume 1. Hillsdale, NJ: Erlbaum, 1980.

Sanacore, J. "Metacognition and the Improvement of Reading: Some Important Links. *Journal of Reading,* May, 706-712, 1984.

Sternberg, R. and Wagner, R. "Understanding Intelligence: What's In It for Education?" Paper submitted to the National Commission on Excellence in Education, 1982.

Whimbey, A. "Students Can Learn to be Better Problem Solvers." *Educational Leadership,* April, 37(7), 1980.

Whimbey, A. and Whimbey, L. S. *Intelligence Can Be Taught.* New York: Bantam Books, 1976.

$\mathcal{S}$ection

The Key Players

"Cogitare is the language we use
to grow intelligent behaviors...
Speaking Cogitare simply means
that we consciously use our
language to evoke thinking in
others...Do you speak Cogitare?"
—*Arthur L. Costa*

What Goes On In Your Head When You Teach?

The following diagram [see Figure 1], which deletes such important concepts as affect, motivation, and perceptual abilities, is an attempt to synthesize many psychologists' and psychobiologists' concepts of human intellectual functioning which can serve as a basis for supervisory decision making. (Being well aware of the limitations of reducing to such a crude model so complex and elegant a concept as the human intellect, this attempt is approached with all due humility.)

The purpose of supervision for intelligent teaching would be to enhance the teacher's innate capacity for using these intellectual functions.

Based on the model [in Figure 1], information taken in is constantly being interpreted in terms of what is already known. If the new information can easily be understood with familiar knowledge in storage, no problem or challenge exists (Assimilation). If, however, the new information cannot be explained or resolved with the knowledge in short- or long-term memory, a discrepancy is perceived and the information must be processed, action taken to gather more information to resolve the discrepancy, and the ultimate resolution tested for its "fit" with reality (Accommodation). Thus, a problem may be defined as some stimulus or challenge, the response to which is not readily apparent.

The supervisor's role, then, is crucial as a mediator of intelligent behavior. To stimulate the use of those skills, the supervisor calls attention to discrepancies and poses problems intended to invite more than a memory-type response. To assist a teacher in the resolution of these problems, the supervisor's questions and statements can be designed to elicit specific cognitive functions which produce data, relationships, and generalizations which can be employed to resolve the problem.

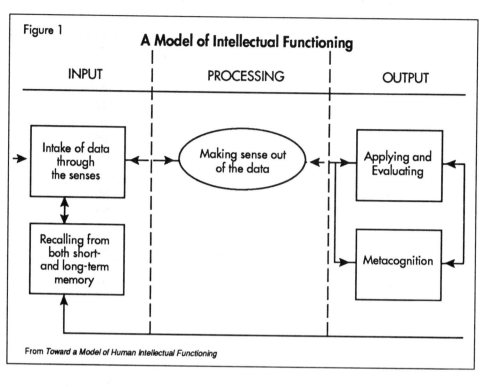

Figure 1

A Model of Intellectual Functioning

INPUT | PROCESSING | OUTPUT

Intake of data through the senses

Making sense out of the data

Applying and Evaluating

Recalling from both short- and long-term memory

Metacognition

From *Toward a Model of Human Intellectual Functioning*

Based on this model, we can recast this information processing system into the thought processes of instruction. Basically there are four that roughly correspond to those in the model of thinking above. They are:

I. Planning (The Preactive Stage)

II. Teaching (The Interactive Stage)

III. Analyzing and Evaluating (The Reflective Stage)

IV. Applying (The Projective Stage)

Planning consists of all those intellectual functions performed during that calmer period prior to instruction. *Teaching* includes all those multiple decisions made during the immediacy and spontaneity of the teaching act. They are probably more intuitive and unconscious than the rational decisions of the planning phase. *Analyzing and Evaluating* consists of all those mental processes used to reflect upon, analyze, and judge the teaching act performed in the past. These, too, are probably performed in a more relaxed state and involve "autocriticism" or the ability to stand away from one's self and contemplate one's own intellectual functioning—a uniquely human act. *Applying* involves learning from experience. As a result of the evaluation and analysis phase, commitments are made to use what was learned from the evaluation of teaching in future teaching activities or actions. It involves abstracting from the teaching experience and carrying forth those generalizations to future situations. Each of these four phases of instruction are examined in depth in the following pages.

I. Planning—
The Preactive Stage.

Psychologists have found that the human intellect has a limited capacity for handling variables. Miller (1956) described this as "M-Space" or Memory Space. He found that the human being has a capacity for handling and coordinating on the average of seven different variables, decisions, or disparate pieces of information at any one time (plus or minus two). This assumes the person has attained the Piagetian stage of formal operations. Not all adults have achieved this stage, however. Therefore, we find that in an average adult population, some may be able only to handle four or so.

It has been found that when humans approach the limits of their capacity, a state of stress begins to set in as if to feel a "loss of control" because the maximum number of variables controllable is being reached. Much intellectual energy appears to be invested in techniques and systems to simplify, reduce, and select the number of variables with which the intellect has to deal. Planning helps to reduce this stress.

During planning a teacher can describe cues—definitions of acceptable forms of student performance for learning and thus simplify judgments about appropriate and inappropriate student behaviors. The teacher can select potential solutions, back-up procedures, and alternative strategies for those times when a learning activity needs to be redirected, changed, or terminated (Newell and Simon 1972). Planning is useful because it causes "thought experiments" during which a teacher can mentally rehearse activities to help anticipate possible events and consequences.

Planning calls upon a teacher to view the learning from a student's point of view. It allows the teacher to imagine how this lesson will be perceived and received by the students. Therefore, superior teachers have the capacity to overcome their "ego-centrism" as they are able to place themselves in the position of the learner and view the lesson from multiple perspectives.

Superior teachers seem to have the capacity to operate under two or more classification systems simultaneously. Basically, this means that they can teach toward both immediate and long-range goals simultaneously; they perceive relationships between the day-to-day student behaviors and their cumulative progress toward long-range educational outcomes; and they can prioritize goals and objectives so that they know which student behaviors to reinforce and which to ignore.

Planning a teaching strategy requires task analysis—both structural and operational. Structural analysis is the process of breaking down the content into its component parts while operational analysis involves a seriation of events into a logical order or sequence (Clark and Yinger 1979).

Thus, planning may well include the most important decisions teachers make since this is the design phase upon which rest the other three phases. Planning basically involves four components (Shavelson 1976, p. 393).

1. *Developing descriptions of students' learning that are to result from instruction.* These are predicted in explicit or observable student behaviors. Zahorik (1975), found this to be of low priority, however.

2. *Identifying the student's present capabilities or entry knowledge.* This information about student abilities is drawn from such sources as previous teaching/learning experiences, data from school records, test scores, and clues from previous teachers, parents, counselors, etc. (Shavelson 1977; Borko, Cone, Russo, and Shavelson 1979).

3. *Envisioning the characteristics of an instructional sequence or strategy which will most likely move the students from their present capabilities toward the immediate and ultimately the long-range instructional outcomes.* This sequence is derived from whatever

theories or models of teaching, learning, or motivation the teacher has adopted.

4. *Anticipating a method of evaluating outcomes.* The outcomes of this evaluation provide a basis for decisions about the design of the next cycle of instruction.

To handle this "information overload" teachers probably synthesize much of this information into "hypotheses" or best guesses about student readiness for learning. They estimate the probability of successful student behavior as a result of instruction (Coladarchi 1959, p. 3-6).

During the planning phase, a wealth of information can be brought to bear because the teacher has the time and lack of pressure to call it from memory. Planning may be done in a formal setting—thinking, writing, and devoting attention to it; or informally, such as while driving to work, washing dishes, upon awakening, etc. The unpressured planning phase is in sharp contrast to the interactive phase of teaching when teachers must respond quickly to the immediate demands of the situation without time to reflect before acting.

This information plays a central role in the decisions teachers make about an overall teaching strategy, including short-range and long-term objectives of instruction, the content and materials to be used, the arrangement of classroom space and social groupings, the time that will be devoted to the several activities, and the acceptability of student performance.

II. Teaching—
The Interactive Stage

O.J. Harvey (1966) described teaching as the second most stressful profession. When a teacher is in the process of constantly interacting with students, he or she is under great pressure and often in a state of uncertainty. This has great influence on the types of decisions a teacher makes (Raiffe 1970). Thus, while the decision steps in the planning phase model [see Figure 2] are similar to those decisions in the interactive stage of teaching, the decisions made during teaching may be either unconscious, spontaneous, planned, or a mixture of each. They are probably modifications of those decisions made during the planning phase. These modifications, however, are made on the spur of the moment. Factors which influence decisions made during interaction are probably not as well defined and as thoroughly considered as alternative teaching strategies and the consequences of each. Insufficient data about students' readiness for learning may be observed or recalled.

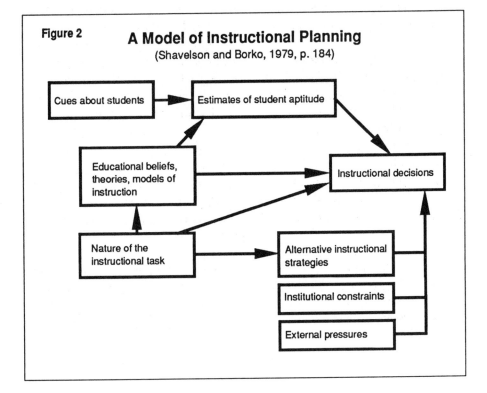

Figure 2 — A Model of Instructional Planning
(Shavelson and Borko, 1979, p. 184)

A teaching strategy is a plan of action. It might be defined in part as a sequentially ordered set of teacher behaviors designed to produce a desired student outcome. Keeping the planned strategy in mind while teaching allows the teacher a backdrop against which to make temporal and comparative judgments and to assess the readiness for more or different learnings. For example, during the beginning of a lesson much emphasis may be placed upon structuring the task and motivating students to become curious, involved, and focused. Later in the sequence, recall types of thinking might be stressed to review previously learned information and to gather data to be considered later. Still later, higher level thinking might be invited (Doyle 1979, p. 54).

Thus, the teacher must make temporal decisions as to when and how fast to move through the steps in the sequence. When are students properly motivated? How much data should be input? When is there an adequate data base on which to predict successful thinking if a higher-level question were to be asked? In the interaction of teaching, a teacher is constantly questioning, probing, observing, and interpreting students' behaviors and making decisions about moving ahead in the sequence or remaining at the present step longer. This sequence of decisions might be diagrammed as in Figure 3. (Each of the diamond shaped boxes represents a decision.)

To handle this "information overload" teachers probably synthesize much of this information into "hypotheses" or best guesses about student readiness for learning. They estimate the probability of successful student behavior as a result of instruction (Coladarchi 1959, p. 3-6).

Thus, a teacher may ask a question as a means of yielding diagnostic information about a student. That information is analyzed in the teacher's mind and a decision made as to which next teacher behavior should be chosen. Should the student's response be praised, extinguished, clarified, and extended? Superior teachers not only know how to ask a range of questions, they also know when to ask them. They know how to select from a repertoire of teacher behaviors and how to predict the outcomes when each is used. Keeping a strategy in mind helps in making these decisions. Without a strategy, classroom interaction is unfocused, random, and chaotic.

A teaching strategy also provides a "screening mechanism" by which teachers can select the relevant and often subtle cues out of the myriad signals that a classroom full of students sends. In order to manage the continual flow of events in the interaction of teaching, the teacher must constantly scan the classroom environment and be alert to cues coming from students. These cues provide an information feedback system on which decisions are based.

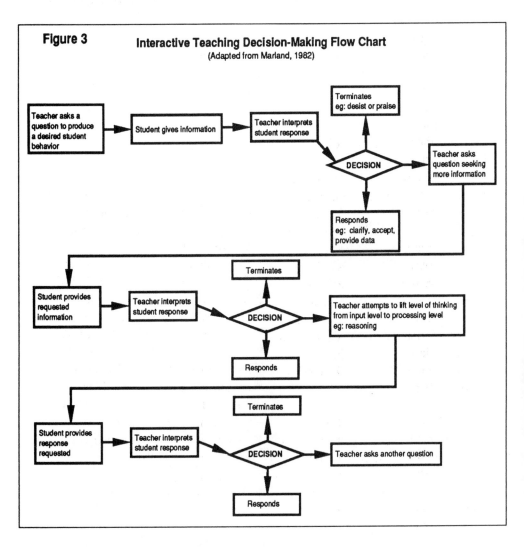

Figure 3   **Interactive Teaching Decision-Making Flow Chart**
(Adapted from Marland, 1982)

As mentioned earlier, however, the human intellect can take in and deal with only a limited amount of data. Information from students is constantly being received through the senses, but teachers' conscious processing of this information can only be directed to a selected number of task-relevant cues. With a strategy in mind, task-relevant cues are noticed more rapidly.

After the teacher sees or hears a particular student behavior (cue), he or she interprets it by either assigning from memory or constructing a particular meaning for it. He or she then either designs or calls from past experience the most appropriate teacher behavior to use in response to that student. It is found that teachers possess impressively large amounts of data and perceptions about students. Teachers seldom, however, check on the accuracy of their interpretations about students' cognitive and affective states. The validity of these interpretations and the appropriateness of the next behavior to be used might, therefore, be questionable (Marland 1982).

Interpretations are also made regarding students with special needs (e.g., disadvantaged, upset, ill, etc.). Thus, teachers often apply compensatory principles in making "special interpretations" for target students. These interpretations may result in unusual teacher behaviors such as praise, granting special favors, using students or their work as models, etc.

Thus, teachers can monitor a classroom for cues which are both conscious and unconscious. Cues are also constantly being received through nonconscious pathways. These cues often "build up" over time and can have great emotional relevance.

Such emotional cues can disrupt conscious information processing. Teachers try to restrain their impulsivity by avoiding strong emotional reactions to classroom events, since emotion tends to preempt attention. Thus, restraint of impulsive or emotional reactions becomes an efficient strategy to reserve the limited capacity for consciously processing the immediate tasks of making classroom decisions (Doyle 1970, p. 58). Superior teachers

probably control their emotional, impulsive reactions to events in (and out) of the classroom.

Routines and management systems are especially helpful in dealing with the information-processing demands of the immediacy, spontaneity, and unpredictability of classroom interaction. Routines reduce the need to attend to the abundance of simultaneous cues from the classroom environment.

Routinizing classroom procedures helps to make the teacher's task more feasible and the students' behavior more predictable. Superior teachers develop routine systems for dealing with many of the classroom management functions (e.g., taking roll, distributing papers and books, forming groups, passing to recess, etc.), as well as having systematic lesson designs (e.g., spelling, math drills, etc.) and teaching strategies (e.g., questioning sequences, structuring, etc.). When a teacher has established routines, cues that signal discrepancies and abnormalities can be attended to rather than having to deal with all student behaviors all the time (Doyle 1979, p. 61-63).

III. Analyzing And Evaluating (The Reflective Stage)

Analyzing involves collecting and using understandings derived from the comparison between actual outcomes and the intended outcomes *(Behavioral Objectives)* of instruction. If there is great similarity between those behaviors that were predicted during the planning stage and those behaviors that were observed during the interaction stage, then there is a "match" and no discrepancy exists (Assimilation). If, on the other hand, there is a mismatch between student behaviors observed and student behaviors intended, a discrepancy exists which must be resolved or explained (Accommodation). Thus, reasons are given to explain this discrepancy; cause and effect relationships are drawn between instructional situations and behavioral outcomes (Barr 1971).

Evaluating involves judging the worth of these decisions made during the planning and interactive phases (Shavelson 1976, p. 400-402). During evaluation, some value is placed on the quality of the thinking that the teacher performed before and during teaching. The ability to self-evaluate is what Binet called "autocriticism" (Whimbey 1976, p. 116-130). A uniquely human intellectual capacity is our ability to stand apart from, contemplate, and evaluate our own actions. This ability involves a conscious awareness of self-interacting with the real world. It is a teacher's inclination to be aware of their own thinking while they are deciding (Introspection) and to reflect upon their thinking after they've decided (Retrospection) (Clark and Yinger 1979).

Superior teachers seem to have an internal, rather than external, locus of control. It is one thing for a supervisor to judge the learning outcomes of a teacher's lesson, but what about teachers' estimates of their own success? (Harootunian and Yarger 1981). Teachers may dismiss or distort information that indicates that students did not learn as a result of their teaching strategy. Teachers may not be entirely rational when they are faced with the possibility that their lesson did not produce desired results; they may be more concerned about maintaining a consistent self-image.

Some studies bear out this point: teachers give themselves credit when there is student improvement, but place blame elsewhere when performance is inadequate. Teachers attribute increase in performance to themselves, but attribute decreases in performance to the environment. (Classroom observers, however, were much less likely to attribute improvement to the teacher and more likely to attribute decreases to the teacher and to student motivation.) (Shavelson 1976, p. 402).

Thus, teachers who are insecure, or who have low self-esteem, may allow biases to enter their interpretations. Superior teachers, who possess a positive self-image, are more likely to "own" or hold themselves responsible for the outcomes of teaching—whether high or low achievement. *Locus of Control*, therefore, refers to the location where the responsibility for outcomes is placed. Teachers can either assume responsibility for their own actions, or they can place the blame on external forces: parents, genetics, previous teachers, textbooks, students' laziness, etc. (Rohrkemper 1982).

IV. Applying
(The Projective Stage)

Knowing when to decide seems to be a cognitive skill of teaching. This comes about through experience. Experience alone, however, is not enough unless meaning is ascribed to it and it is applied. Experience then must be compared, differentiated, categorized, and labeled. Such a conceptual system provides a relationship among the many classroom events and the probability of unlikely events. Such a system allows the teacher to recognize and interpret classroom events, departures from routines, and novel occurrences. Thus, the teacher can predict the consequences of possible alternatives and directions of activities. Without this conceptual system, the classroom remains a mass of chaos and confusion. (Since this knowledge comes through experience, it explains why the demands on inexperienced teachers is so intense; their knowledge is both being tested and constructed at the same time.) (Doyle 1979, p. 65-74).

Superior teachers, therefore, reflect upon, conceptualize, and apply understandings from one classroom experience to the next. As concepts about teaching accumulate, teachers become more routinized, particularized, predictable, and refined.

Concepts and relationships derived from the analysis and evaluation stage can be extrapolated in making future decisions in planning and interactive teaching. During this application stage, teachers formulate hypothetical statements or future plans. Hypotheses might be characterized by "iffy" thinking. "If I were to do this lesson again, I would . . ." Future-oriented thinking must include such statements as "From now on I'm going to . . ." or "Next time I'll plan to . . ."

Thus, superior teachers seem to make commitments to change their behaviors and strategies based upon self-analysis—gathering and processing the data from their experience and knowledge and projecting forth those relationships to future situations. This step closes the instructional cycle as it serves as a basis for future planning which is in Stage I.

In Summary

Many of the cognitive or intellectual processes involved in the four components of the instructional act have been examined. To be sure, this does not include all the kinds of teacher decisions or intellectual processes teachers make. It is, however, an attempt to refocus the energies of the supervisor from only the overt behaviors of teaching to include the inner thinking processes of teaching.

References

Barr, R. and Brown, V.L. "Evaluation and Decision Making" in *The Reading Teacher.* Vol. 24, No. 4, 1971.

Berliner, D. "The Half-full Glass: A Review of the Research on Teaching" in *What We Know About Teaching,* P. Hosford, Editor. Alexandria, Virginia: ASCD, 1984.

Blumberg, A. *Supervisors and Teachers: A Private Cold War.* Berkeley: McCutchan Publishers, 1974.

Borko, H. et al. "Teachers' Decision Making" in *Research On Teaching,* D. Peterson and H. Walberg, Editors. Berkeley: McCutchan Publishers, 1979.

Clark, C. and Yinger, R. "Teachers' Thinking" in *Research On Thinking.* P. Porterson and H. Walberg, Editors. Berkeley: McCutchan Publishers, 1979.

Coladarachi, A.P. "The Teacher as Hypothesis Maker" in *California Journal of Instructional Improvement.* Vol. 2, March, 1959.

Costa, A. *The Enabling Behaviors: A Course Syllabus.* San Anselmo, CA: Search Models Unlimited, 1982.

Doyle, W. "Making Managerial Decisions in Classrooms" in *1979 Yearbook of the National Society for the Study of Education, Part II.* D. Duke, Editor. Chicago: University of Chicago Press, 1979.

Glickman, C. *Developmental Supervision: Alternative Approaches to Helping Teachers Improve Instruction.* Alexandria, Virginia: ASCD, 1980.

Harootunian, B. and Yarger, G. "Teachers' Conceptions of Their Own Success" in *ERIC Clearinghouse on Teacher Education.* No. S017 372, February, 1981.

Harvey, O. J. "System Structure, Flexibility and Creativity" in *Experience, Structure and Adaptability.* O. J. Harvey, Editor. New York: Springer, 1966.

Harvey, O. J.; Kelley, H. H.; and Shapiro, M. "Reactions to Unfavorable Evaluations of the Self-made by Other Persons" in *Journal of Personality,* Vol. 25, June 1957.

Jackson, P. *Life in Classrooms.* New York: Holt, Rinehart and Winston, 1968.

Kerlinger, F. and Pedhazur, E. "Educational Attitudes and Conception of Desirable Traits of Teachers" in *American Educational Research Journal,* Vol. 5, 1978.

Marland, P.W. Paper presented at the Conference on Thinking, University of the South Pacific, Suva, Fiji, January, 1982.

Miller, G. A. "The Magical Number Seven, Plus or Minus Two: Some Limits in Capacity for Processing Information" in *Psychological Review,* 1963.

Morine, G. and Vallance, E. "A Study of Teacher and Pupil Perceptions of Classroom Interaction" A technical report of the beginning teacher evaluation study. San Francisco: Far West Laboratory for Educational Research and Development, 1976.

Newell, A. and Simon, H. *Human Problem Solving.* Englewood Cliffs, NJ: Prentice-Hall, 1972.

Raiffa, H. *Decision Analysis: Introductory Lectures on Choices Under Uncertainty.* Reading, PA: Addison Wesley, 1970.

Rohrkemper, M. "Teacher Self-Assessment" in *Helping Teachers Manage Classrooms.* D. Duke, Editor. Alexandria, Virginia: ASCD, 1982.

Ryan, K. "Stages of Teacher Growth" in Presentation at the Annual Conference of the Association of Supervision and Curriculum Development, 1979.

Shavelson, R. "Teacher Decision Making" in *The Psychology of Teaching Methods 1976 Yearbook of the National Society for the Study of Education, Part I.* Chicago: University of Chicago Press, 1976.

Shavelson, R. "Teacher Sensitivity to the Reliability of Information in Making Pedagogical Decisions" in *American Educational Research Journal,* Vol. 14, Spring 1977.

Shavelson, R. and Borko, H. "Research on Teachers' Decisions in Planning Instruction" in *Educational Horizons,* Vol. 47, Spring 1977.

Whimbey, A. and Whimbey, L.S. *Intelligence Can Be Taught.* New York: Bantam Books, 1976.

Zahorick, J. "Teachers' Planning Models" in *Educational Leadership,* Vol. 33, 1975.

———— 🙣 ————

Do You Speak Cogitare?

Embedded in the vocabulary, inflections, and syntax of the language of adults lie the cognitive processes derived by children. Research over many years has demonstrated the close, entwined relationship of language and thought. From birth, children imitate the sounds, then words, phrases and thought patterns of the significant adults who mediate their environment (Vygotsky 1962; Feuerstein 1980; Flavell 1977).

Through interaction with adults during children's formative, early years, they develop the foundations of thought that endure throughout their lifetimes. Environments and interactions that demand and provide models of more complex language and thought contribute to the ability to handle complex thinking processes as children mature (Sternberg and Caruso 1985).

In the past two decades there has been a significant transformation of the American family. With increases in the amount of time passively spent watching television, both parents working or traveling, single-parent families, children giving birth to children, and "latch-key kids," family life sometimes lacks meaningful verbal interaction. Some children are parentally and therefore linguistically deprived. When children enter school lacking the complexity of language and thought needed to master academic demands, they are often disadvantaged (Bronfenbrenner 1975).

With the recent educational emphasis on the education of the intellect, we wish to have students acquire the ability and inclination to perform discrete thinking skills, cognitive processes, and problem-solving strategies (Ennis 1985). Success in school and future careers is dependent upon autonomous application of the skills of problem solving, innovation, and decision making.

Educators often assume that students know how to perform these skills.

They are asked daily by the teacher or the instructional materials, for example, to summarize, to draw conclusions, to infer, to categorize, or to compare. Yet these processes are often omitted as essential skills to be taught. Students may be at a loss to know what to do when the task is to classify a word list, to infer the author's intent in a reading passage, or to draw conclusions from a set of data.

Adults in the child's environment can subtly and carefully compose language using selected syntax, vocabulary, and inflection to stimulate, engage, and practice desired cognitive processes in children. Teachers can consciously select key cognitive terminology so that students will encounter those words in common, everyday dialogue. We can formulate questions to cause students to exercise certain cognitive functions. We can provide data which students must interpret for themselves. We can remain non-judgmental so that children must make their own judgments. It is believed that if adults will monitor their own language for the embedment of cognitive terminology and if they will seize opportunities for thinking in the day-to-day interactions of the classroom, a positive effect will result in students' cognitive structures which, in turn, will produce an increase in their academic success.

What follows are some suggestions for monitoring our language and some ways to enhance children's thinking during the daily interactions of classroom life.

Thinking Words

Teachers are often heard to admonish students to think: "Think hard!" Students are sometimes criticized for not having the inclination to do so: "these kids just go off without thinking."

The term "think" is a vague abstraction covering a wide range of mental activities. Two possible reasons why students fail to engage in it are: 1) the vocabulary is a foreign language to them, and 2) they may not know how to perform the specific skills that term implies. When adults speak *cogitare*—using specific cognitive terminology and instruct students in ways to perform those skills – they will be more inclined to use them (Astington and Olson 1990).

As children hear these cognitive terms in everyday use and experience the cognitive processes that accompany these labels, they will internalize the words and use them as part of their own vocabulary. Teachers will also want to give specific instruction in those cognitive functions so that students possess experiential meaning along with the terminology (Beyer 1985).

Figure 1

Instead of saying:	**Speak *cogitare* by saying:**
"Let's look at these two pictures"	"Lets *compare* these two pictures."
"What do you think will happen when...?"	"What do you *predict* will happen when...?"
"How can you put into groups...?"	"How can you *classify*...?"
"Lets work this problem."	"Let's *analyze* this problem."
"What do you think would have happened if..."	"What do you *speculate* would have happened if..."
"What did you think of this story?"	"What *conclusions* can you draw about this story?"
"How can you explain...?"	"What *hypothesis* do you have that might explain...?"
"How do you know that's true?"	"What *evidence* do you have to support...?"
"How else could you use this...?"	"How could you *apply* this...?"

Discipline

When disciplining children, teachers often make the decisions about which behaviors to desist and which to reinforce. Teachers can speak *cogitare*—posing questions that cause children to examine their own behavior, search for the consequences of that behavior, and choose more appropriate actions for themselves (Bailis and Hunter 1985). For examples, see Figure 2.

Figure 2

Instead of saying:	**Speak *cogitare* by saying:**
"Be quiet!"	"The noise you're making is disturbing us. Is there a way you can work so that we don't hear you?"
"Sarah, get away from Shawn!"	"Sarah, can you find another place to do your best work?"
"Stop interrupting!"	"Since it's Maria's turn to talk what do you need to do?"
"Stop running!"	"Why do you think we have the rule about always walking in the halls?"

111

Discussions with children about appropriate behavior, classroom and school rules, and courtesy will be necessary if they are to learn appropriate alternatives. Then, when they occasionally forget, they can go back in their memory for what was learned. Soon they will monitor their own behavior—an important dimension of metacognition (Costa 1984).

Provide Data, Not Solutions

Sometimes we rob children of the opportunity to take charge of their own behavior by providing solutions, consequences, and appropriate actions for them. If adults would merely provide data as input for children's decision making, we can cause them to act more autonomously, to become aware of the effects of their behavior on others, and to become more empathic by sensing the verbal and non-verbal cues from others. We can speak *cogitare* by giving data, divulging information about ourselves, or sending "I" messages.

Some children, of course, will be unable to detect these data as cues for self-control. In such cases, we may have to step in and provide more specific directions for appropriate behavior. We can start, however, by allowing the student to control him or herself.

Classroom Management

When communicating instructions on how to perform a task, teachers can *speak cogitare* which will cause students to analyze a task, decide on what is needed, then act autonomously. Too often teachers may give all the information so that students merely perform the task without having to infer meaning. (For examples see Figure 4.)

Figure 3

When children:	Speak *cogitare* by saying:
Make noise by tapping their pencil	"I want you to know that your pencil tapping is disturbing me."
Interrupt	"I like it when you take turns to speak."
Whine	"It hurts my ears."
Are courteous	"I liked it when you came in so quietly and went right to work."
Chew gum	"I want you to know that gum-chewing in my class disturbs me."

112

Figure 4

Instead of saying:	**Speak *cogitare* by saying:**
"For our field trip, remember to bring spending money, comfortable shoes, and a warm jacket."	"What must we remember to bring with us an our field trip?"
"The bell has rung; it's time to go home. Clear off your desks, slide your chairs under the desk quietly, and line up at the door."	"The bell has rung. What must we do to get ready to go home?"
"Get 52 cups, 26 scissors, and 78 sheets of paper. Get some butcher paper to cover the desks."	"Everyone will need two paper cups, a pair of scissors, and three sheets of paper. The desk tops will need to be protected. Can you figure out what you'll need to do?"
"Remember to write you name in the upper right hand corner of your paper."	"So that I easily can tell who the paper belongs to, what must you remember to do?"
"You need to start each sentence with a capital and end with a period."	"This sentence would be complete with two additions. Can you figure out what they are?"

Probing For Specificity

Oral language is filled with omissions, generalizations, and vaguenesses. Our language is conceptual rather than operational, value-laden, and sometimes deceitful. Speaking *cogitare* causes others to define their terms, become specific about their actions, make precise comparisons, and use accurate descriptors (Laborde 1984).

Being alert to certain vague or unspecified terms cues our need to speak *cogitare* — the language of specifics. These vague terms fall into several categories:

1) Universals, including "always," "never," "all," or "everybody";

2) Vague action verbs – "know about," "understand," "appreciate";

3) Comparators such as "better," "newer," "cheaper," "more nutritious";

4) Unreferenced pronouns – "they," "them," "we";

5) Unspecified groups – "the teachers," "parents," "things";

6) Assumed rules or traditions including "ought," "should," or "must."

When such words or phrases are heard in the speech or writings of others, we speak *cogitare* by having them specify, define, or reference their terms.

Figure 5

When we hear:	**Speak *cogitare* by saying:**
"He *never* listens to me."	"Never?" "Never, ever?"
"*Everybody* has one."	"Everybody?" "Who, exactly?"
"*Things* go better with..."	"Which things specifically?"
"Things *go* better with..."	"Go? Go – how specifically?"
"Things go *better* with..."	"Better than what?"
"You *shouldn't* do that..."	"What would happen if you did?"
"The *parents*..."	"Which parents?"
"I want them to *understand*..."	"What exactly will they be doing if they understand..."
"This cereal is *more nutritious*"	"More nutritious than what?"
"*They* won't let me..."	"Who is 'they'?"
"*Administrators*..."	"Which administrators?"

"Critical thinkers" are characterized by their ability to use specific terminology, to refrain from overgeneralization, and to support their assumptions with valid data. Speaking *cogitare* by having children use precise language develops those characteristics (Ennis 1985).

Metacognition

Thinking about thinking begets more thinking (Costa 1984). Having children describe the mental processes they are using, the data they are lacking, and the plans they are formulating causes them to think about their own thinking – to metacogitate. When teachers speak *cogitare* they cause the covert thought processes that students are experiencing to become overt. Whimbey refers to this as "Talk Aloud Problem Solving" (Whimbey 1985).

Figure 6

When children say:	Speak *cogitare* by saying:
"The answer is 43 pounds, 7 ounces."	"Describe the steps you took to arrive at that answer."
"I don't know how to solve this problem."	"What can you do to get started?"
"I'm comparing..."	"What goes on in your head when you compare?"
"I'm ready to begin."	"Describe your plan of action."
"We're memorizing our poems."	"What do you do when you memorize?"
"I like the large one best."	"What criteria are you using to make your choice?"
"I'm finished."	"How do you know you're correct?"

As teachers probe students to describe what's going on inside their head when thinking is taking place, students become more aware of their own thinking processes; and, as they listen to other students describe their metacognitive processes, they develop flexibility of thought and an appreciation that there are several logical ways to solve the same problem.

Presuppositions

Language may be interpreted in terms of its "surface" meaning and its "structural" meaning. Surface meaning refers to the word definitions, syntax, semantics, grammar, verb forms, modifiers, etc. Structural meaning, on the other hand, refers to the subtle nuances, connotations, feelings, and images conveyed by the words.

A presupposition is a hidden, covert, implicit meaning buried within the structure of the statement or sequence of language. For example: "Even Richard could pass that course." Hidden with the sub-structure of this sentence are several implied meanings: that Richard is not too bright a student, and further, that the course must be a cinch! Neither of these pieces of information is overtly present in the surface structure of the sentence. It does not say, "Even Richard, who is not too bright a student, could pass that course which is a cinch!" The implicit meaning or presupposition, however, is blatant (Elgin 1980).

115

Over time, these messages "seep" into children's awareness below the level of consciousness. Often they are unaware that such verbal violence is being used against them. They feel hurt or insulted in response to language that may sound, on the surface, like a compliment. Interestingly, people behave in response to other's perceptions of them – they behave as if they are expected to behave that way. Over time, these negative presuppositions accumulate and produce in students poor self-esteem and a negative self-concept as a thinker. Their negative behavior follows.

Interestingly, we can also use *positive* presuppositions. Teachers can purposely select language to convey a positive self-concept as a thinker: "As you plan your project, what criteria for your research report will you keep in mind?" Notice the positive presuppositions: that you are planning, that you know the criteria for the research report, that you can keep them in your mind, and that you can metacognitively apply them as you work.

Teachers never purposely set out to deprecate students' self-esteem. Unconsciously, however, these negative presuppositions may creep into the language of classroom interaction. Teachers who speak *cogitare* will monitor their own language for their positive rather than negative presuppositions.

Figure 7

Instead of saying:	Speak *cogitare* by saying:
"Why did you forget to do your assignment?"	"As you plan for your assignment, what materials will you need?"
"Why don't you like to paint?"	"We need you to paint a picture to add to our gallery of outstanding artists."
"Did you forget again?"	"Tell us what you do to help you remember."
"When will you grow up?"	"As we grow older, we learn how to solve these problems from such experiences."
"Here, I'll give you an easier puzzle; then you'll be successful."	"As the puzzles get more difficult, how will you use planning like this again?"

The Study Of Cogitare

Like any language, *cogitare* is dynamic. It can be analyzed, refined, transmitted to others, created, and can became archaic. Students, too, can explore the linguistic structure of *cogitare.*

We can, for example, focus on word clusters or syntactical cues within the language that give clues as to what cognitive operations those words evoke. This is sometimes referred to as discourse analysis. It includes such cognitive processes as concept formation, relationship identification, and pattern recognition.

For example, students can search for relationships as a way of "linking" information. They can find the word or word cluster that cues the thinking process of that relationship. This process is called "relationship identification." It requires students to:

- identify separate ideas that are related within a sentence.

- identify the type of relationship between the ideas (addition, comparison, causality, sequence, or definition).

- identify the linguistic cue for the performance of that cognitive relationship (and, or, but, after, while, etc.).

Cognitive Process Type Of Relationship Example Of Linguistic Cue

Addition
Two ideas go together in same way. "He is intelligent *and* he is kind."

Comparison
Common attributes are shared. "Shawn *and* Sarah *both* play the violin."

Contrast
Two ideas don't go together. "He is healthy *but* he doesn't exercise."

Causality
One event causes another. "Peter went home *because* his work was finished."

Sequence
One event happens before, during, or after another event. "He went home *then* he went to the library."

It is believed that teaching students to be alert to the cognitive process embedded in written and spoken language can help them become aware of their own language and thought. It can help them decode the syntactic, semantic, and rhetorical signals found in all languages, and it can help them integrate the complex interaction of language, thought, and action (Marzano and Hutchins 1985).

117

In Summary

Our language is a tool. As a tool we can use it to enhance others. Speaking *cogitare* simply means that we consciously use our language to evoke thinking in others by:

1. using specific cognitive terminology rather than vague abstract terms.

2. posing questions that cause children to examine their own behavior, search for the consequences of that behavior, and choose more appropriate actions for themselves.

3. giving data, divulging information about ourselves, or sending "I" messages so that students must "process" the information.

4. causing students to analyze a task, decide on what is needed, then act autonomously.

5. causing others to define their terms, become specific about their actions, make precise comparisons, and use accurate descriptors.

6. causing the covert thought processes that students are experiencing to become overt (metacognition).

7. employing positive presuppositions to enhance self-concept as a thinker.

8. helping children study and become alert to the cues in the structure of language which evoke thought processes.

By asking questions, selecting terms, clarifying ideas and processes, providing data, and withholding value judgments we can stimulate and enhance the thinking of others. *Cogitare* is the language we use to grow intelligent behavior.

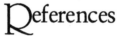

References

Astington, S. and Olson, D. "Metacognition and Metalinguistic Language: Learning to Talk About Thought." *Applied Psychology: An International Review*, 39(1), 77-87, 1990.

Bailis and Hunter, M. "Do Your Words Get Them to Think?" *Learning*, August, 14(1), 1985.

Beyer, B. "Practical Strategies for the Direct Teaching of Thinking Skills." In A. L. Costa (Ed.), *Developing Minds: A Resource Book for Teaching Thinking*. Alexandria, VA: Association for Supervision and Curriculum Development, 1985.

Bronfenbrenner, U. *Influences on Human Development*. Hillsdale, IL: Erlbaum, 1975.

Costa, A. "Mediating the Metacognitive." *Educational Leadership,* November, 42, 3, 57-62, 1984.

Elgin, S. *The Gentle Art of Verbal Self Defense.* United States: Dorset Press, 1980.

Ennis, R. "Goals for a Critical Thinking Curriculum." In A. Costa (Ed.), *Developing Minds: A Resource Book for Teaching Thinking.* Alexandria, VA: Association for Supervision and Curriculum Development, 1985.

Feuerstein, R. *Instrumental Enrichment.* Baltimore, MD: University Park Press, 1980.

Flavell, J. *Cognitive Development.* Englewood Cliffs, NJ: Prentice-Hall, 1977.

Laborde, G. *Influencing with Integrity.* Palo Alto, CA: Syntony Press, 1984.

Marzano, R. and Hutchins, C. L. *Thinking Skills: A Conceptual Framework.* Aurora, CO: Mid-continent Regional Educational Laboratory, 1985.

Sternberg, R. and Caruso, S. "Practical Modes of Knowing." In E. Eisner (Ed.), *Learning and Teaching the Ways of Knowing. 84th Yearbook of the National Society for the Study of Education.* Chicago, IL: University of Chicago Press, 1985.

Vygotsky, L. S. *Thought and Language.* Cambridge, IL: Massachusetts Institute of Technology Press, 1962.

Whimbey, A. "Test Results for Teaching Thinking." In A. Costa (Ed.), *Developing Minds: A Resource Book for Teaching Thinking.* Alexandria, VA: Association for Supervision and Curriculum Development, 1985.

———— ✿ ————

Cognitive Coaching: A Strategy For Reflective Teaching

Arthur L. Costa and Robert J. Garmston

Cognitive Coaching is a marriage of the professional experiences of Art Costa and Bob Garmston. Art had been working with a supervision model long before we came together in the early 1980s. Art's background was in cognition and intellectual development, having studied with Jean Piaget, Jerome Bruner, Hilda Taba, J. Richard Suchman, Reuven Feuerstein, and others. Bob's background was parallel, having also been influenced by Suchman, and by Caleb Gattegno, Fritz Perls, Carl Rogers, Abraham Maslow, and, most recently, John Ginder. Cognitive Coaching is a blend of our two perspectives.

Assumptions

Cognitive Coaching is based upon some fundamental beliefs about teaching and human growth and learning. We believe that all human beings are capable of change, that we continue to grow cognitively throughout our lifetime, and that we all possess a vast reservoir of untapped potential.

We believe that teaching cannot be reduced to a formula or a recipe. There is an enormous amount of information today about specific instructional behaviors which produce certain student learnings. In such process-product research studies, however, there were always certain "outlier" teachers who did not use these behaviors but obtained good results in student learning. Still other teachers who *did* use all the behaviors produced poor results. Thus, while we have knowledge about teaching, we do not have certainty about teaching.

Another fundamental assumption is that a teacher's observable classroom performance is based upon internal, invisible skills – thought processes that drive the overt skills of teaching. We subscribe to Shavelson's (1973) proposition that the basic teaching behavior is decision making, and we build our assumptions on the research of Peterson and Clarke (1986), who describe a four-phase cycle of instructional decision making in which

121

teachers engage before, during, and after classroom instruction. The first phase comprises all the thought processes which teachers perform prior to classroom instruction—the planning phase. The second includes those mental functions performed during the teaching act—the interactive phase. The third is the reflective phase in which teachers look back to compare, analyze, and evaluate the decisions that were made during the planning and teaching phases. Finally, there is an application phase in which teachers abstract from what has been learned during their own critical self-reflection and then project those learnings to future lessons. They then cycle back to the planning phase.

A fourth assumption is that enlightened, skillful colleagues can significantly enhance (mediate) a teacher's cognitive processes and therefore the teacher's perceptions and decisions which produce the resulting teaching behaviors.

Goals

Cognitive coaches keep clearly in mind three major goals or outcomes of employing this process: trust, learning, and autonomy.

The first goal is trust – trust in the process, trust in each other, and trust in the environment. Both parties in the coaching relationship need to trust and respect each other, realizing that neither person needs to be "fixed."

Coaches believe that people have the inner resources to achieve excellence. Increasingly, they place their faith in the coaching process. As the coach and teacher work together in a non-threatening relationship, they realize the intent of this process is to grow intellectually, to learn more about learning, and to mutually increase their capacity for self-improvement. Cognitive coaches work toward long-range gains rather than fixing a lesson immediately. Occasionally, with a new teacher, it may be necessary to save the lesson, but that is not generally what we are after. Another aspect of trust is in the school environment. The culture of the workplace often signals norms and values which may be more influential on teacher performance than are teacher training, staff development, or coaching (Frymier 1987). Thus, the effective coach is also interested in creating, monitoring, and maintaining a stimulating, mediational, and cooperative environment deliberately designed to enhance continued intellectual growth.

A second goal is learning. We believe that all learning requires an engagement of and a transformation of the mind. To learn anything well—a golf swing, a poem, a new computer program, or a different way of teaching—all require thought. Coaches, therefore, are skillful in engaging the teacher's intellect, in maintaining the teacher's access to his or her higher cognitive functions, and in employing tools and strategies which will enhance teachers' perceptions and expand their frames of reference.

The third, and most profound of the goals, is that of developing cognitive autonomy. We give coaches and teachers a mental coaching map: a protocol of specific objectives for the preconference and postconference. Once they have internalized that map, they can be totally present with each other. Coaches can then use their relationship skills, knowing that trust and rapport in the relationship is paramount if the teacher is to be able to think. As a result of cognitive coaching over time, our intent is to develop teachers' ability to self-monitor, to self-analyze, and to self-evaluate. Indeed, the ultimate purpose of Cognitive Coaching is to modify teachers' capacities to modify themselves.

Coaching Competencies

To accomplish these goals, five non-judgmental mediational competencies of the coach are required. The coach must remain non-judgmental throughout the coaching process so that people can think without fear of being judged. When people feel judged, their thinking shuts down.

The first ability is posing carefully constructed questions intended to challenge the teacher's intellect. The second process is paraphrasing. According to Carl Rogers, the paraphrase is probably the single most important communication tool and yet the most underused. Paraphrasing communicates that "I am attempting to understand you, therefore I value you." Because it conveys such powerful empathy, its use permits deep and tenacious probing.

The third is the skill of probing for specificity, clarity, elaboration, and precision: "Which students specifically?" or "What criteria will you be using to assess the accuracy of student responses?" or "What else were you considering when you reorganized the assignment," for example. Probing invites and promotes deeper, more detailed thinking that results in greater consciousness and more analytical, productive decision making.

The fourth skill is using silence. As we know, wait time has been found by Mary Budd Rowe (1986) and others to be a significant linguistic tool leading to more creative and reflective thinking.

A fifth competency is that of collecting data and presenting it objectively. Skillful coaches assist the teacher in designing strategies, or they draw from their own repertoire of data-gathering techniques relevant to the teacher. The coach and teacher can then examine the data in a literal and non-judgmental way (Costa, D'Arcangelo, Garmston, and Zimmerman 1988).

Thus, the cognitive coaching process is much like a Socratic dialogue. The better thinkers coaches are, the more capable they are of producing and stimulating thinking in others.

The Cognitive Coaching Process

Cognitive Coaching is a model used for supervision or peer coaching. It is equally appropriate for administrators, department chairs, resource teachers, mentors or peers: anyone in a helping relationship. It is *not* evaluative. As a supervisory process, it is very close to the original clinical supervision model developed by Anderson and Goldhammer (1969) and Cogan (1973). Their intent, which has been distorted in some recent "clinical supervision" models, was to provide a collegial relationship that supports teachers in becoming critically self-reflective about their work. We have simply overlaid their process with a "cognitive," developmental dimension.

Cognitive Coaching includes a preconference, a lesson observation, and a postconference. Thus, the format of the coach's role is compatible with the four phases of thought that effective teachers (or any competent, thoughtful problem solvers for that matter) perform.

We attach great importance to the preconference. Without it, teachers are more likely to be anxious about the observation, and coaches will lack the teacher's valuable guidance for their data collection. A second, more compelling reason for the preconference is that we believe planning is the most important of all the instructional thought processes. The quality of the plan affects the quality of all that follows. One critical mental process during planning is to identify lesson outcomes and literally envision what students will be doing during the lesson that will indicate whether or not they have achieved those objectives. Effective teachers, like winning athletes, mentally rehearse what they will be doing to produce desired results prior to performance (Garfield 1986).

In the preconference the coach invites the teacher to elaborate on the learning goals and to describe how the teacher will ascertain, during the lesson, whether students are learning. This may be difficult for some teachers who conceive the judgment of students' learning to be determined at a later time, when a test is given. Our assertion is that by then it's too late. The teacher needs to monitor the cues indicating student success during the lesson. Skillful coaching assists the teacher in imagining, elaborating, and devising strategies to monitor such formative cues from students.

The teacher is asked about his or her instructional strategies for reaching these outcomes. In addition, the coach asks what he or she should pay attention to and collect data about in the lesson that will support the teacher's growth. The coach does this by becoming another set of eyes for the teacher and a mediator of the teacher's processing of his or her own teaching experience.

During the lesson itself the coach collects only that data the teacher requested during the preconference. Such observations may focus on student performance indicating goal achievement, on-task behavior, or a particular student's problem behavior. The coach may also be requested to collect data about techniques which teachers are striving to perfect: wait time, questioning strategies, proximity, movement, clarity of directions, etc.

The postconference is frequently begun with an open-ended question such as, "How do you feel the lesson went?" We say "frequently" because, while coaches have certain conferencing objectives they intend to meet, the dialogue is more individualized and Socratic than it is a recipe. An open invitation allows the teacher to decide how he or she will enter this conversation and begin self-assessment. The next question may be something like, "What are you recalling from the lesson that's leading you to those inferences?" This question focuses on another important cognitive function of teaching – monitoring and recalling what happened during a lesson. This differs from some coaching systems in which the coach simply feeds back what was observed and recorded on a taped script. Because the ultimate goal of Cognitive Coaching is self-modifica-

tion, teachers need to develop the ability to monitor their own and their students' behaviors and to recall what happened in the lesson. Data collection is fundamental to their self-analysis and self-coaching. Processing the data from the lesson enables teachers to reconstruct and analyze what went on while they were teaching to make the teaching experience intelligible.

Next, the teacher may be asked to interpret the data – to compare desired with actual outcomes: "How did what happened in the lesson compare with what was desired?" The teacher may also be asked to infer what he or she observed in the lesson in terms of cause-effect relationships. The teacher then may be asked – if it is appropriate – about some teaching strategies and techniques that in hindsight he or she might have done differently that might have produced alternate results. Finally, the teacher is asked to project and apply what has been learned: "How will you use these insights in future lessons or in other aspects of your work?" Notice the positive presuppositions that are embedded in these questions. This is a process concerned with self-motivation and self-directed growth. The job of the coach is to support the teacher in this natural mental journey.

Outcomes Of Cognitive Coaching

Teachers and coaches report that they are deriving enormous satisfaction from using this process. Coaches make comments such as, "A teacher came up with alternatives that would have never occurred to me," or "A teacher who has not been very reflective is telling me that he now is watching himself teach, almost like he had a camera on himself, and that when he catches himself in old patterns, he now employs alternatives." Administrators describe how they use the coaching process with each other as they talk through plans for staff development training or a crucial parent meeting. Teachers report that the process is enjoyable and exciting, that it makes them think, and that as a result of the coach's modeling higher level questions, probing, and paraphrasing, they are using those same non-judgmental behaviors with students!

Can such invisible skills of teaching be taught and learned? We believe they can. Adults can continually modify their cognitive capacities. Teachers in staff development workshops often tell us that their awareness and command of cognitive skills has increased – through their learning how to cognitively coach one another. This happens more often, however, in training programs and with those models of supervision which focus primarily on the thinking that underlies instructional behaviors, rather than on the behaviors of teaching alone.

We have learned—and this is consistent with everything we know about good staff development—that

the kind of changes toward which we strive do not happen quickly. A district should make a three-year commitment that begins with a seven-day training program. We ask the district to plan a support system that assists cognitive coaches in their application of the knowledge, skills, and attitudes that were acquired in the workshop (Garmston 1987). This application phase requires a sustained focus where two aspects are monitored: frequency and mutations. Frequency is important both to help the coach internalize skills and to produce maximum benefits for teachers. Studies have demonstrated the obvious; the more engagement, the higher the benefits. The benefits are transformational in nature when the frequency of coaching of up to six or seven times a year is achieved (Foster 1989; Garmston 1989; and Garmston and Hyerle 1988). After that, the cognitive skills of self-coaching are in place—and the frequency of coaching may decrease. Mutation monitoring is also important. There is a tendency, left unchecked, to mutate back toward evaluative behavior from the coach. This is natural given the history and environments of many schools. Trained resident leadership in each district or region can help sustain the integrity of the cognitive coaching process by serving as a "meta-coach," by networking with other cognitive coaches, brainstorming solutions to problem situations, renewing coaching skills, and challenging ever-increasing coaching complexity.

A final phase we see evolving in districts is policy change. In our experience, policy change usually occurs after there is a critical mass of teachers and coaches who are experimenting with the process. A needed change in policy becomes increasingly apparent as the principles of cognitive coaching are internalized and applied. We begin to observe a shift in district practices from teacher evaluation to goal clarification and coaching, from competition to cooperation, from conformity to creativity, and from control to empowerment. We've observed a dissatisfaction with existing curriculum and a shift from acquiring more content to a focus on developing students' intellectual processes. We sense that cognitive coaching can be the impetus for developing the school as a home for the mind, an intellectual ecology where all the school's inhabitants' intellects are mediated (Costa 1991).

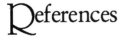

References

Anderson, R. and Goldhammer, R. *Clinical Supervision.* New York: Holt Rinehart & Winston, 1969.

Cogan, M. *Clinical Supervision.* Boston, MA: Houghton Mifflin, 1973.

Costa, A. "The School as a Home for the Mind." In A. Costa (Ed.), *Developing Minds: A Resource Book for Teaching Thinking.* Alexandria, VA: Association for Supervision & Curriculum Development, 1991.

Costa, A.; D'Arcangelo, M.; Garmston, R.; and Zimmerman, D. *Another Set of Eyes: Conferencing Skills.* Video tapes and trainer's manual in ASCD's Supervision series. Alexandria, VA: Association for Supervision and Curriculum Development, 1988.

Costa, A. and Garmston, R. "Supervision for Intelligent Teaching." *Educational Leadership,* 42 (5), 70-80, 1985.

Foster, N. *The Impact of Cognitive Coaching on Teachers' Thought Processes As Perceived by Cognitively Coached Teachers in the Plymouth-Canton Community School District.* Doctoral Dissertation, Michigan State University, Detroit, MI, 1989.

Frymier, J. "Bureaucracy and the Neutering of Teachers." *Phi Delta Kappan,* September, 69(1), 9-14, 1987.

Garfield, C. *Peak Performers: The New Heroes of American Business.* New York, NY: William Morrow and Company, Inc., 1986.

Garmston, R. "How Administrators Support Peer Coaching." *Educational Leadership,* 44(5), 18-26, 1987.

Garmston, R. "Cognitive Coaching and Professors' Instructional Thought." *Human Intelligence Newsletter,* 10(2), 3-4, 1989.

Garmston, R. and Hyerle, D. *Professors' Peer Coaching Program: Report on a 1987-88 Pilot Project to Develop and Test a Staff Development Model for Improving Instruction at California State University*, Sacramento, CA, August, 1988.

Peterson, P. and Clark, C. "Teachers' Thought Processes." In C. Wittrock (Ed.), *Handbook of Research on Teaching*. Third Edition, American Educational Research Association, 255-296, 1986.

Rowe, M. B. "Wait Time: Slowing Down May be a Way of Speeding Up!" *Journal of Teacher Education*, January/February, 23, 43-49, 1986.

Shavelson, R. "The Basic Teaching Skill: Decision Making." R&D Memorandum No. 104, Stanford, CA: Stanford University School of Education, Center for R&D in Teaching, p. 18, 1973.

———— ❧ ————

The Administrator's Role In Enhancing Thinking Skills

School effectiveness research supports what many educators intuitively know: the principal has a strong influence on the curriculum implemented, the instructional strategies employed, and thus, on student achievement.

Nationwide efforts to infuse thinking skills into the curriculum, to include them in instructional strategies, and to assess schools' success in teaching thinking are capturing the attention and energies of boards of education, curriculum committees, and departments of education. Obviously, the role of principals in this endeavor is critical. Their behaviors are symbolic for staff members, students, and the community.

This chapter clarifies the principal's role and suggests how principals can exert their crucial influence in enhancing students' full intellectual functioning and development. Principals can approach this goal by (1) creating intellectually stimulating school conditions for staff and students, (2) using available resources to support a cognitive curriculum, and (3) modeling rational practices.

Creating Intellectually Stimulating School Conditions

If teachers are expected to teach for thinking, they need an environment in which their intellectual processes are stimulated. One role of the principal, therefore, is to create a school atmosphere that invites teachers' highest intellectual functioning (Sprinthall and Theis-Sprinthall 1983). There are many ways principals can create intellectually stimulating environments. For instance, they can:

1. Involve teachers, parents, and students in decision making.
Teachers in effective schools have opportunities to participate in making decisions that affect them. Mandates

from above are among the greatest deterrents to thinking. Principals must encourage, facilitate, and protect teachers' rights to:

- pursue self-studies.

- develop goals.

- plan personal staff development.

- prioritize which thinking skills to emphasize.

- select their own instructional materials.

- invent methods to determine their own effectiveness.

- determine indicators of student growth.

- share and suggest solutions to problems.

As teachers participate in making decisions that affect them, the likelihood that those processes will infiltrate their classrooms greatly increases.

2. *Employ collegial supervision rather than evaluation.*

Another way to inhibit thinking is to make value judgments about teachers' competencies, potentials, and ideas. Value judgments detract from motivation and produce stress (Lepper and Greene 1978). Under stress, the brain's creative, analytical functions are extinguished and replaced with conformity (MacLean 1978). Instead, withholding judgments and viewing teaching and learning as a continual problem-solving, creative method of inquiry build trust and challenge teachers to become experimental hypothesis makers. Supervision thereby becomes "brain compatible" (Hart 1983; Costa and Garmston 1985).

3. *Avoid recipes.*

It is tempting to describe and evaluate the act of teaching in "five steps, four factors, and seven variables." Obviously, teaching and learning the complex strategies of higher-level thinking are more lengthy and dignified than that. Teaching *by the number* is as creative as painting by the number. Participants must capitalize on this complexity, find richness in this confusion, and avoid simplistic answers.

4. *Explicate the dream.*

Principals of effective schools have a vision of what their schools can become. They constantly assess all programs, each decision, and every new direction in order to help achieve that vision. In their pursuit of excellence, they strive to be thoughtful, rational, innovative, and cooperative. In addition, principals should seize every opportunity to articulate, refine, and magnify this vision by:

- openly discussing it with the faculty, community, fellow administrators, and central office staff.

- illuminating instruction that illustrates it.

- finding materials that are consistent with it.

- organizing classrooms to better achieve it.

Not only do these activities help clarify principals' intuitive perceptions, but they also make a strong public statement about their values.

5. Constant reminders.

"Thought is Taught at Huntington Beach High" emblazons one school's memo pads. "The 'HOTS' (Higher-Order Thinking Skills) Committee will meet in the teachers' room at 3:30" resounds from another school's loudspeaker. A brightly painted banner exclaiming "Thursday is for Thinking" decorates one wall of the teachers' room as a not-so-subtle souvenir of their commitment to plan at least one thinking skills lesson each week. Lesson plan books list Bloom's taxonomical levels of thinking on the covers. "Just a Minute, Let Me Think" is the slogan on the bulletin board in yet another school's foyer. In a staff lounge, a butcher paper scope-and-sequence chart displays skill activities entered by each teacher at each grade level for each subject area. These are but a few of the many innovative ways principals strive to keep their staff members thinking about thinking.

Using Available Resources To Support Thinking

Resources are usually defined in terms of time, space, energy, and money. How principals allocate these limited resources is yet another significant expression to staff members, students, and the community of their value systems.

Most obvious is the principal's commitment of financial resources for thinking skills programs by purchasing materials and hiring consultants to assist the faculty in curriculum and staff development, sending staff members to conferences and workshops, and securing substitutes to facilitate peer observation.

Securing financial grants from local industries, philanthropic organizations, and national, state, and local education agencies is one way to increase this often limited resource.

Because time and energy are an administrator's most precious commodities, parceling them out wisely is crucial to their effectiveness. The following suggestions should attract administrators' highest priorities.

1. Monitor instructional decision making.

Once the staff has defined how to effectively teach thinking, these indicators may be monitored in the instructional decisions teachers make, such as:

- planning lessons that include cognitive objectives.

- sequencing teaching strategies according to levels of thought.

- selecting instructional materials that stimulate problem solving.

- organizing the classroom for discussion of ideas.

- developing learning activities that provoke thinking.

- evaluating student growth in thinking abilities.

In these ways, administrators convey to teachers that *instruction* is the mechanism by which thought is taught; if instruction is improved, thinking will improve correspondingly.

2. Coordinate the curriculum.

Possessing a broad curriculum purview, principals are in a good position to effectively monitor the relationship between teachers' instructional decisions and the district's philosophical goals. They can search for ever-increasing complexity and abstraction of thinking required in learning activities at each grade level, coordinate resources with other schools in the district or community, and evaluate the long-range cumulative effects of cognitive instruction.

3. Use precious faculty time to think and discuss thinking.

Too often, faculty meeting time is relegated to managerial tasks and information transmission. Discussing thinking as a total faculty, or in department- or grade-level meetings, is time well spent. Agenda items can include inviting teachers to:

- report what they have learned from thinking skills courses, staff development activities, or research.

- describe successes and problems in teaching for thinking.

- discuss which thinking skills to focus on this year.

- demonstrate instructional techniques that provoke thinking.

- compare how they include thinking in each subject area.

- describe how children increase the complexity of their intellectual skills throughout their development.

- review and select materials to enhance thinking.

- discuss ways to support each other's teaching with concurrent instruction (thinking across the curriculum).

- invent alternative ways to assess students' growth in thinking abilities.

- relate school goals to district priorities.

4. *Secure parental support.*

Parents probably have the most effect on children's abilities and inclinations for mental development. Concerned parents model thinking; their language engages differential cognitive structures. Often what we do in schools to teach thinking is remedial for those students whose parents do not provide this mediation.

Principals are the primary link between schools and the community. They have the opportunity to involve parents in decision making, interpret school programs to the community, and educate parents in their dominant role as mediators of their children's cognitive development.

Some parents believe that schools should teach only the basics. They may judge modern education in terms of their experience as students—during a time when the value of thinking was not necessarily recognized. Principals can help parents enhance their aspirations for their children stressing that reasoning is a basic for survival in the future, critical thinking is required for college entrance and success, cognitive processes are prerequisite to mastery in all subjects, and career security and advancement are dependent on innovation, insightfulness, and cooperation.

Many parents appear to be realizing that reasoning is the fourth "R," and there is a definite trend toward increased parental concern for children's cognitive development (Gallup 1984). Principals should engage parents to search for ways to encourage children to use thinking by stimulating their interest in school and learning, environmental issues, time and money planning, and so on.

Time and energy invested in parental education pay high dividends. Elementary school administrators may wish to involve their school psychologists and nurses in enhancing parental effectiveness. Secondary and college-level school administrators may consider including parenting classes in their curriculum. Possible offerings include instruction in such cognitively related understandings as: promoting language development, experiential stimulation, parent-child communication skills, good nutrition, child growth and development, rational approaches to discipline, supervising homework, providing home environments conducive to cognitive development, and modeling appropriate adult behaviors.

5. *Enhance personal thinking skills.*

If any time and energy remain, principals themselves may wish to participate in staff development activities and learn more about cognitive education by: learning to distinguish among the many programs available, considering what to look for in teacher-student classroom interaction, studying how to apply criteria to the selection of instructional materials, understanding more about brain functioning, and increasing their own cognitive skills of problem solving, creativity, research, and cooperative planning.

Modeling In The Principal's Own Behavior

Imitation is the most basic form of learning. Emerson is often quoted as saying, "What you do speaks so loudly they can't hear what you say." Thus, when problems arise in the school, the community, and the classroom, the principal must be seen solving those problems in rational, thoughtful ways. If not, the principal may unknowingly undermine the very goals of curriculum to which commitment is sought. Evaluation of a teacher's or program's effectiveness may be performed by the very person who is rendering the program ineffective. Principals should emulate those rational competencies desired in students and taught by teachers through:

1. Withholding impulsivity.

The environment of the school principal is analogous to living in a popcorn popper. It's easy to become tense, fatigued, and cognitively overloaded. Effective principals, however, develop self-awareness and biofeedback strategies to combat stress and to cope with irritating problems through patience, rationality, and poise.

2. Demonstrating empathy for others.

One of the highest forms of mental ability is empathy. Behaving empathically requires overcoming one's own egocentricity, detecting another's subtle emotional and physical cues, and perceiving a situation from another's point of view—a complex of cognitive processes. When dealing with parents, staff members, colleagues, and students, the administrator who demonstrates empathy will model the most potent intellectual process.

3. Metacognition.

Metacognition is our ability to formulate a plan of action, monitor our own progress along that plan, realize what we know and don't know, detect and recover from error, and reflect upon and evaluate our own thinking processes. Administrators demonstrate metacognition when they publicly share their planning strategies, admit their lack of knowledge but describe means of generating that knowledge, and engage others in deliberating, monitoring, and evaluating problem-solving strategies.

Metacognition seems to be an attribute of effective problem solvers. Administrators can model effective problem solving by demonstrating their awareness of, discussing, and then inviting feedback and evaluation of their own problem-solving abilities (Costa 1984).

4. Cooperative decision making.

Democratic principals realize that their intellectual power multiplies when they draw on the power of others. They value group thinking in decisions facing staff members. This requires attitudes such as withholding judgment, coping with ambiguity, flexible thinking, tentativeness, evaluating alternatives, seeking consensus, taking another person's point of view, and employing hypothetical, experimental thinking. These are the same attributes of critical thinking and problem solving that we want teachers to instill in students.

5. Believing that children can think.

School effectiveness research indicates that teachers' and administrators' expectancies of student performance are correlated with achievement. Likewise, in programs of cognitive education, our expectancies become apparent. In many schools, however, children with low I.Q. scores are thought incapable of higher-level thought. Some schools employ thinking programs only for the gifted. Some children are "excused" from thinking because of the supposed inadequacies of home environment, culture, socio-economic level, or genetic makeup.

Indeed, those students who are reluctant to think—who recoil from mental activity because it's "too hard"—are the ones who need it most.

Modern cognitive theorists reject the notion of a static and unchanging I.Q. Rather, they adopt a dynamic theory of multiple intelligences that can be nurtured and developed throughout a person's life. Administrators must demonstrate the belief that, with proper mediation and instruction, *all* children can continue to increase their intellectual capacities (Gardner 1983; Feuerstein 1980; Whimbey and Whimbey 1875).

References

Costa, A. "Mediating the Metacognitive." *Educational Leadership* 42 (November 1984): 57-62.

Costa, A. and Garmston, R. "Supervision for Intelligent Teaching." *Educational Leadership* 42 (February 1985): 70-80.

Feuerstein, R. *Instrumental Enrichment.* Baltimore: University Park Press, 1980.

Gallup, G. "The 16th Annual Gallup Poll of the Public's Attitudes Toward the Public Schools." *Phi Delta Kappan* 66 (September 1984).

Gardner, H. *Frames of Mind.* New York: Basic Books, 1983.

Hart, L. *Human Brain, Human Learning.* New York: Longman, 1983.

Lepper, M. and Greene, D. *The Hidden Costs of Rewards.* Hillsdale, NJ: Lawrence Erlbaum Associates, 1978.

MacLean, P. "A Mind of Three Minds: Educating the Triune Brain." In *Education and the Brain, 77th Yearbook of the National Society for the Study of Education.* Edited by J. Chall and A. Mirsky. Chicago: University of Chicago Press, 1978.

Sprinthall, N. and Theis-Sprinthall, L. "The Teacher as an Adult Learner: A Cognitive Developmental View." In *Staff Development, 82nd Yearbook of the National Society for the Study of Education.* Edited by G. Griffin. Chicago: University of Chicago Press, 1983.

Whimbey, A. and Whimbey, L. *Intelligence Can Be Taught.* New York: E. B. Dutton and Co., 1975.

———— ❧ ————

Section IV

The Evaluation Dilemma

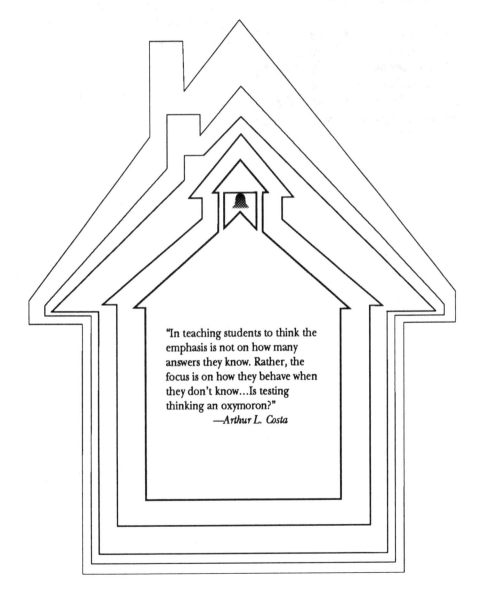

"In teaching students to think the emphasis is not on how many answers they know. Rather, the focus is on how they behave when they don't know...Is testing thinking an oxymoron?"
—*Arthur L. Costa*

Is Testing Thinking An Oxymoron?

The task of aligning the curriculum is usually composed of three major decisions: establishing the purposes, outcomes, goals, or objectives of the educational enterprise, be it at the classroom, school, district, state, or national level; designing the delivery system by which those goals will be achieved, including instructional design, materials selection, allocation of time, and placement of learnings; and developing procedures for monitoring, collecting evidence of, and evaluating the achievement of our goals as a result of employing our delivery system.

In the curriculum alignment process, sound educational practice dictates that the first group of decisions (the goals) needs to drive the system. Unfortunately, like it or not, what is inspected is what is expected. The traditional use of norm-referenced, standardized tests have dictated what should be learned (the goals) and have influenced how they should be taught (the delivery).

As our youth confront the demands of the 21st century, educators are realizing that new goals are becoming increasingly apparent as survival skills for their future and the future of our democratic institutions. These goals include the capacity for continued learning: how to learn; cooperation and team building; communicating with precision in a variety of modes; coping with disparate value systems; solving problems requiring creativity and ingenuity; enjoyment of resolving ambiguous, discrepant, and paradoxical situations; dealing with an overabundance of technologically produced information; taking pride in the craftsmanship of their products; and building personal commitment to larger organizational and global goals.

These new goals are needed to drive the new curriculum alignment in the restructured schools of the future. The delivery system—curriculum materials, instructional strategies, and school organization *and* the curriculum alignment decision-making processes

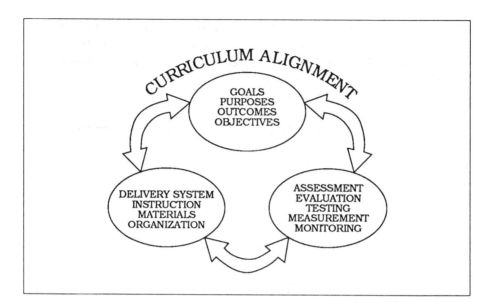

employed—needs to embody these goals not only for students but for all of the school's inhabitants.

Likewise, our methods of assessment must be transformed to become more consistent with our new goals. We can't employ product-oriented assessment techniques to assess the achievement of process-oriented goals. Norm-referenced, standardized test scores provide us a more static number reflecting the achievement and performance of isolated skills at a particular moment in a lifetime. Thinking, however, is in a dynamic state of flux: learning from experience, reacting emotionally to a situation, feeling powerful in problem solving, and being energized by learning— "entering the zone"— so to speak. Thus testing thinking may indeed be an oxymoron.

Recently, we are witnessing a nationwide surge to go "beyond the bubble." State departments of education are providing leadership by experimenting with and advocating innovative methods: writing samples, materials manipulation, open-ended-multiple-answer questions, and portfolios (California State Department of Education Conference, Sacramento, October 16, 1989). Teachers are learning how to more skillfully collect data about student performance of thinking skills through direct observation, group projects and discussions, anecdotal records, recording critical incidents, keeping checklists, journal writing, and engaging students in extended projects.

Such innovative methods are more authentic for several reasons. First, they resemble the situation in which real problem solving and creativity is demanded and actually performed rather than being contrived. Second, they are more meaningful to teachers in order to diagnose students abilities. Third, they take place during the interaction of instruction rather than being delayed until the instructional act is completed. Furthermore, they more immediately provide results to teaching teams to assist them in evaluating the effectiveness of their own curriculum and instructional efforts. Finally, they provide "real-time" feedback to students themselves who are (or who must become) the ultimate evaluators of their own performance.

There are several tasks which educators must now address:

1) educating legislators, the public, parents, and school boards to value and seek these more appropriate and meaningful ways of assessing the new goals of their new schools for the 90s and beyond;

2) equipping teachers with the skills and knowledge of employing new assessment methods; and

3) helping curriculum leaders and administrators orchestrate systematic assessment and monitoring of their students' progress toward these goals.

As educators we must guard against our worst fears, that like the much defiled "government worker," "postal service," or "military intelligence,"

terms such as "educational system," "curriculum change," and "teachers of thinking" may become oxymorons as well.

——— ⁊ ———

Thinking: How Do We Know Students Are Getting Better At It?

When considering how evidence of students' achievement is collected, we most often think of testing—using some form of paper and pencil instrument to determine how many questions a student answers correctly. While there may be some types of thinking that can be assessed in this fashion, we must seek additional means of determining growth in intellectual abilities. In teaching students to think the emphasis is not on how many answers they know. Rather, the focus is on how they behave when they don't know. We are interested in observing how students produce knowledge rather than how they merely reproduce knowledge. A critical characteristic of intellectual ability is not only having information, but knowing how to act upon it.

By definition, a problem is any stimulus, question, or phenomenon, the explanation for which is not immediately known. Thus, student performance is assessed under challenging conditions which demand strategies, insightfulness, perseverance, and craftsmanship to resolve the problem.

Many teachers are unimpressed with standardized tests (Harootunian and Yarger, 1980; Lazar-Morrison, et al., 1980). The results are often unavailable for several weeks or months after administering the test; thinking skills are contaminated by the degree to which students are acquainted with the subject matter; behavior is influenced by the mental and emotional state of the students at the time of testing; performance is subject to the vicissitudes of the situation; scores yield neither diagnostic clues as to how the student derived the answer (metacognition) nor information on how the student processed the data and emotions necessary to arrive at the best answer (cognitive mapping) (Anderson, 1981; Coffman, 1980).

Teachers know that many students are deemed gifted because they are test wise. They also know that other students are often overlooked because they do poorly under testing conditions. While competency may be demonstrated in a single test, effectiveness is demonstrated by sustained performance in a variety of situations which demand the selective and spontaneous use of clusters and linkages of problem-solving strategies rather than singular, isolated behaviors.

As students interact with real life and day-to-day classroom problems, what might teachers search for as indicators that their instructional efforts are paying off? Following are ten suggested characteristics of intellectual growth which teachers can observe and record (Feuerstein, 1980). Keeping anecdotal records of a student's acquisition of these types of behaviors provides more usable information about growth in intellectual behaviors than typical norm-referenced, multiple choice, standardized achievement tests.

1. *Persevering when the solution to a problem is not immediately apparent*

Students often give up in despair when the answer to a problem is not immediately known. We can observe them crumple their papers and throw them away saying, "I can't," or "It's too hard." They lack the ability to analyze a problem, to develop a system, structure, or strategy of problem attack.

Thinking students grow in their ability to use alternative strategies of

problem solving. If one strategy doesn't work, they know how to back up and try another. They realize that the theory or idea must be rejected and another employed. They have systematic methods of analyzing a problem, knowing ways to begin, knowing what steps must be performed, what data need to be generated or collected. This is what is meant by perseverance.

2. *Decreasing Impulsivity*

Often students blurt the first answer that comes to mind. sometimes they shout out an answer, start to work without fully understanding the directions, lack a plan or strategy for approaching a problem, or make immediate value judgments about an aide before fully understanding it.

As students become less impulsive, we can observe them decreasing the number of erasures on their papers, gathering much information before they begin a task, taking time to reflect on an answer before giving it, making sure they understand directions before beginning a task, listening to alternative points of view, and planning a strategy for solving a problem.

3. *Flexibility In Thinking*

Some students have difficulty in considering alternative points of view, or dealing with more than one classification system simultaneously. Their way to solve a problem seems to be the only way. They are more interested in knowing whether their answer is correct or not, rather than being challenged by the process of finding the answer. They are unable to sustain a process of problem solving and finding the answer over time, and therefore avoid ambiguous situations. They have a need for certainty rather than an inclination for doubt.

As students become more flexible in their thinking they can be heard considering, expressing, or paraphrasing another person's point of view or rationale. They can state several ways of solving the same problem and can evaluate the merits and consequences of two or more alternate courses of action. When making decisions they will often use such words as "however," "on the other hand," "if you look at it another way . . ." or "John's idea is . . ., but Mary's idea is . . . ."

4. Meta-Cognition: The Ability To Know What We Don't Know

Some people are unaware of their own thinking processes. They are unable to describe the steps or strategies they use during the act of problem solving. They cannot transform into words the visual images held in their minds. They seldom evaluate the quality of their own thinking skills.

We can determine if students are becoming more aware of their own thinking as they are able to describe what goes on in their head when they think. When asked, they can list the steps and tell where they are in the sequence of a problem-solving strategy. They can trace the pathways and blind alleys they took on the road to a problem solution. They can describe what data are lacking and their plans for producing those data (Sternberg and Wagner, 1982).

5. Checking For Accuracy

Students are often careless when turning in their completed work. When asked if they have checked over their papers, they might say, "No, I'm done." They seem to feel little inclination to reflect upon the accuracy of their work, to contemplate their precision, or to take pride in their accomplishments. Speed of getting the assignment over with surpasses their desire for craftsmanship.

We can observe students growing in their desire for accuracy as they take time to check over their tests and papers, as they grow more conscientious about precision, clarity, and perfection. They go back over the rules by which they were to abide, the models they were to follow, and the criteria they were to employ to confirm that their finished product matches exactly.

6. Problem Posing

One of the distinguishing characteristics between humans and other forms of life is our ability to find problems.

Yet, students depend on others to solve problems, to find answers, and to ask questions for them (Brown, 1983).

Over time, we want to see a shift from teachers asking questions and posing problems, toward students asking questions and finding problems for themselves. Furthermore, the types of questions students ask should change and become more specific and profound. For example:

We seek an increase in requests for data to support conclusions and assumptions. Such questions as, "What evidence do you have . . .?" or "How do you know that's true?" will be heard.

We want to hear more hypothetical problems. These are characterized by "iffy" type questions: "What do you think would happen if . . .," or "If that is true, then . . .?"

We want students to recognize discrepancies and phenomena in their environment and to inquire into their causes: "Why do cats purr?" "How high can birds fly?" "Why does the hair on my head grow so fast, but the hair on my arms and legs doesn't?" "What would happen if we put the salt water fish in the fresh water aquarium?" "What are some alternative solutions to international conflicts other than wars?"

7. Drawing On Past Knowledge And Experiences

Too often students begin each new task as if it were being approached for the very first time. Teachers are often dismayed when they invite students to recall how they solved a similar problem previously and students don't remember. It's as if they never heard of it before, even though they had the same type of problem just recently. It is as if each experience is encapsulated and has no relationship to what has come before or what comes afterward.

Thinking students are able to abstract meaning from one experience and carry it forth to apply it in the next experience. Students can be observed growing in this ability as they are heard saying "This reminds me of . . . " or "This is just like the time when we . . . " They explain what they are doing now in terms of analogies with or references to previous experiences. They call upon their store of knowledge and experience as sources of data to support, theories to explain, or processes to solve each new challenge.

8. Transference Beyond The Learning Situation

Probably the ultimate goal of teaching thinking skills is for the students to apply school-learned knowledge to real-life situations and to content areas beyond that in which it was taught. Yet, we find that while students can pass mastery tests in mathematics, for example, they often have difficulty in deciding whether to buy six items for $2.38 or seven for $2.86 at the super-market.

When parents and other teachers report how they have observed students thinking at home or in other classes, we know students are transferring. Parents, for example, may report increased interest in school, more planning in their child's use of time and finances, in increased organization of their room, their books, and their desks at home.

We might hear, for example, the social studies teacher describe how a student used a problem-solving strategy which was originally learned in the science class. We might hear the wood shop teacher tell how a student volunteered to plan to measure accurately before cutting apiece of wood: "measure twice and cut once," an axiom learned in the math class.

9. *Precision Of Language*
Some student's language is confused, vague, or imprecise. They describe attributes of objects of events with such non-specific words as "weird," "nice," or "OK." Names for objects are such as "stuff," "junk," or "things." Their sentences are often punctuated with "ya know," "er," and "uh."

As students' language becomes more precise, they can be heard using more descriptive words to distinguish

attributes. They will use more correct names, and when universal labels are unavailable, they will use analogies such as "crescent shaped" or "like a bow tie." They will speak in complete sentences, clarify, and operationally define their terminology. Their speech will become more concise, descriptive, and coherent.

10. *Enjoyment Of Problem Solving*
Some children and adults avoid problems. We often hear them saying something like, "These types of thinking games turn me off," "I was never good at these brain teasers," or "Go ask your father; he's the brain in this family." Many people never enrolled in another math class or other "hard" academic subjects after they didn't have to in high school or college. Many people perceive thinking as hard work and therefore recoil from situations which demand "too much" of it.

We want to observe students moving not only toward an "I *can*" attitude, but also toward an "I *enjoy*" feeling. We will notice students seeking out problems to solve on their own and submit to others. They will make up problems to solve on their own and request them from others. Furthermore, students will solve problems with increasing inde-pendence, without the teacher's help or intervention. Such statements as "Don't tell me the answer, I can figure it out by myself," will indicate growing autonomy.

Conclusion

Assessing thinking through exclusive use of standardized, paper-pencil techniques is inadequate. Each teacher should look for indicators of growing intelligence. Most teachers neither need nor use standardized tests to determine the effectiveness of their teaching for thinking. Significant problem-solving behaviors are displayed and can be observed daily if we know how to recognize them.

As educators, we have the great responsibility of instilling intelligent behaviors in our students. We must teach them to value intelligent and rational action. To do so, we must provide conditions conducive to the practice and demonstration of intelligent behavior. We must believe that all students can continue to grow in their ability to behave more intelligently, and we must have faith in the ability of all humans to become increasingly more gifted. Finally, we must set an example by modeling these intelligent behaviors ourselves (Costa, 1983).

References

Anderson, A., "Testing and Coaching." Paper presented at the annual meeting of the American Association of School Administrators, Atlanta, Georgia, 1981.

Brown, I., *The Art of Problem Posing.* The Franklin Institute Press, Philadelphia, Pennsylvania, 1983.

Coffman, W. E. "Those Achievement Tests—How Useful?" in *Executive Review*, Vol. 1, No. 1, 1980.

Costa, A. "Teaching Toward Intelligent Behavior" in *Thinking The Expanding Frontier.* W. Maxwell, Editor. Franklin Institute Press, Philadelphia, Pennsylvania, 1983.

Feuerstein, R., *Instrumental Enrichment.* Teachers who have taught this program report changes in student behaviors similar to those described herein.

Harootunian, B. and Yarger, D., *Teachers' Conceptions Of Their Own Success.* Eric Clearinghouse on Teacher Education, Washington, DC, No. SP 017372, 1981.

Lazar-Morrison, C. and others, *A Review of the Literature on Test Use.* Center for the Study of Education, Los Angeles, 1980.

Sternberg, R. and Wagner, R., "Understanding Intelligence: What's In It for Educators?" Paper presented to the National Commission on Excellence in Education, July, 1980.

——— ❧ ———

How Do You Know If Thinking Has Been Infused?

"We have infused thinking skills into our curriculum and instruction," the Assistant Superintendent informed me. "Congratulations," I replied. As a devotee of the thinking skills movement, I was immediately impressed and intrigued. I wanted to know more.

"Tell me about it," I inquired. "How do you know that thinking skills have been infused?"

"All of our curriculum guides in every subject area have been built upon Bloom's Taxonomy and all of our teachers have been trained to compose their questions using Bloom's levels of thinking," he replied proudly. "We've done it" (Bloom 1956).

From somewhere in its dim recesses my mind began to audiate a tune: *"Is that all there is?"* That is certainly a valiant start, I thought. But Bloom has been around for thirty-one years. What does it mean when we say, "We've done it?" Does *it* take that long? Somehow

there must be more to *it*. Does educating the intellect relate only to curriculum and instructional issues? Will teaching thinking merely be a fad of the 80s?

I conducted an informal survey of several school principals and district curriculum leadership personnel. "How do you know," I asked, "if thinking has been infused?" The responses I received were varied and included such descriptors as:

- adopting one or more of the major published programs.

- training all teachers in teacher effectiveness, lesson design, and higher-level questioning.

- rewriting tests to include critical thinking.

- identifying, deciding upon, and developing a scope- and sequence-allocated instruction in specific thinking skills and strategies to specific grade levels and subject areas.

While thinking about what I would look for as indicators of infusion, I heard two presentations at the 1987 ASCD National Conference that impressed me: one by Jon Saphier, Director of Research for Better Teaching, Carlisle, Massachusetts; the other by Terence Deal, Professor of Educational Leadership, Peabody School of Education, Vanderbilt University. Both talked about a core value system: Saphier talked about a school's culture; Deal talked about industry's elan. As I listened, I began wondering—what if thinking were the school's core value—what might be some observable indicators that a true intellectual focus has been achieved?

Perhaps our search for infusion is too limited. Thinking skills are not just kid's stuff. If education is to achieve an intellectual focus, then the total school environment must mediate all its inhabitants' intelligent behavior. Building on Saphier and Deal's ideas, I developed a list of twelve indicators. As you consider them, you might assess the degree to which your school district, your school, and your classrooms have infused thoughtful education for all.

1. Collegiality

The essence of collegiality is that people the in school community are working together to better understand the nature of intelligent behavior, how it develops, how it is taught and assessed, and how the total school experience can be organized to better promote growth in learners' intellectual abilities.

Professional collegiality at the district level is evident when teachers and administrators from different schools, subject areas, and grade levels meet to coordinate district efforts in enhancing intelligent behavior across all content areas as well as in district policies and practices. Committees and advisory groups assess staff needs, identify and locate talent, and participate in district level decisions and prioritizing. They support and provide liaison with school site efforts, plan district-wide inservices and articulation to enhance teachers' skills and to develop an aligned, coordinated, and developmentally appropriate curriculum for students.

Materials-selection committees review and recommend adoption of materials and programs intended to enhance students' thinking. Through district-wide networks, teachers share information and materials and teach each other about skills, techniques, and strategies they've learned to be effective.

At the school site, teachers plan, prepare, and evaluate teaching materials. They visit each other's classrooms frequently and give feedback about the relationship between their instructional decision making and the resultant student behaviors. They prepare, develop, remodel, and rehearse lessons, and units of study together.

Teachers and administrators continue to discuss and refine their visions and definitions of thinking and the teaching and evaluation of students' intellectual progress. Child study teams keep portfolios of students' work and discuss individual student's developmental thought processes and learning styles. Instructional problems are explored, and experimental solutions are co-generated. Faculty meetings are held in classrooms where the host teacher shares instructional practices, materials, and videotaped lessons with the rest of the faculty. Teachers sequence, articulate, and plan for continuity and reinforcement of thinking skills across grade levels and subject areas.

Collegiality and collaboration is in evidence in the classroom as well. Students may be observed working together with their "study-buddies," in cooperative learning groups, and in peer problem solving. Students participate in class meetings to establish plans, set priorities, and to assess how well they are growing in their intelligent behaviors.

2. Experimentation And Action Research

Experimentation implies that an atmosphere of risk-taking exists. Data can be generated without fear that it

will be used as a basis for evaluation of their success or failure. Creativity will more likely grow in a low-risk atmosphere (Kohn 1977).

An experimental, risk-taking climate will be in evidence as various published programs and curricula are pilot tested. Evidence is gathered over time and the resulting effects on students are shared.

Teachers become researchers as alternate classroom arrangements and instructional strategies are tested while colleagues observe the resulting student interactions. Experiments are conducted with various lesson designs, instructional sequences, and teaching materials to determine their effects on small groups of students or with colleagues prior to large group instruction.

The classroom climate, too, will foster risk-taking as students experiment with ideas, share their thinking strategies with each other and venture forth with creative thoughts without fear of being judged. Value judgments and criticism are replaced with acceptance of, listening to, empathizing with, and clarifying each other's thinking (Costa 1984).

3. Appreciation And Recognition

Whether it be art work, acts of heroism, or precious jewels, what is valued is given public recognition. Core values are communicated by that which is appreciated. If thinking is valued, it too will be recognized by some expression of appreciation. This is true for students in the classroom, and by teachers and administrators as well.

Some observable school indicators might include teachers being invited to describe their successes and unique ways of organizing for teaching thinking. In faculty meetings teachers share videotaped lessons of which teachers are proud. The positive results of teachers' lesson planning, strategic teaching, and experimentation are showcased.

Some observable classroom indicators might include students being recognized for persevering, striving for precision and accuracy, cooperating, considering another person's point of view, planning ahead, and expressing empathy. Students applaud each other for acts of ingenuity, compassion, and persistence. Positive results of students' restraint of impulsivity are described.

4. High Expectations

"Thinking *is* important, you *can* think, you *will* think, and I'll help you learn to think." There is an inherent faith that *all* human beings can continue to grow and improve their intellectual capacities throughout life—that all of us have the potential for greater giftedness, creativity, and intellectual power.

Some students may perceive thinking as hard work and therefore recoil from

situations which demand "too much" of it. Students, teachers, and administrators realize that learning to use and continually refine their intelligent behavior is the purpose of their education. They continue to define and clarify that goal, and seek ways to gain assistance in achieving that goal.

Mottoes, slogans, and mission statements are observable throughout the classroom, the school, and the district. *"Lincoln Schools Are Thought-full Schools"* is the motto painted on one district's delivery trucks for all the community to see. Bookmarks reminding the community that thinking is the school's goal are distributed to service organizations and the public by the superintendent of Plymouth-Canton, Michigan Public Schools. *"Thought Is Taught At Huntington Beach High"* is emblazoned upon the school's note pads. *"Make Thinking Happen,"* is printed on Calvin Coolidge Elementary School's letterhead stationery in Shrewsbury, Massachusetts. *"Thinking Spoken Here,"* is a constant classroom reminder of Stockton, California history teacher Dan Theile's purpose for students.

Expectancies are communicated when staff members periodically report breakthroughs in their progress toward installing thinking in their schools and classrooms. Superintendents review with administrators their long-range goals and visions and their progress toward including the development of intelligent behaviors in their school's mission. Teachers are invited to share what they've done to enhance student's thinking in the past month. In classrooms journals are kept and students periodically report new insights they are gaining about their own problem-solving strategies.

5. Protecting What's Important

Knowing that thinking is important as a goal, *all* inhabitants of the school believe that their right to think will be honored and protected. This overarching and primary goal is kept in focus as district leaders make day-to-day decisions. This may prove to be difficult as pressures from public and vocal special interest groups distract us from our mission. Our vision may be temporarily obscured by politically expedient and financially parsimonious decisions.

Thinking is valued not only for students, and certificated staff, but for the classified staff as well. A principal of a "thinking school" reported that a newly-hired custodian constantly asked her to check on how well he was cleaning the classrooms and to tell him whether he was doing an adequate job. She decided to help him develop a clear mental image of what a clean classroom looked like and then worked to enhance his ability to evaluate for himself how well the room he cleaned fit that image.

Teachers' rights to be involved in the decisions affecting them are protected and those who do not choose to be involved in decision making are also honored in their choice.

Fads, bandwagons, and other educational innovations which may detract from our intellectual focus are ignored as irrelevant to our central issue. Philosophical discussions, however, are encouraged because they give voice to alternative views. Considering other points of view as expressed in such books as Bloom's *Closing Of The American Mind* (1987), Finn and Ravitch's *What Do Our 17 Year Olds Know?* (1987), Hirsch's *Cultural Literacy* (1987), creates tensions, honors divergent thinking, and expands and refines our vision. Such discussion further verifies the staff's definition of literacy to include modes of thinking and inquiring. It strengthens the staff's commitment to the principle that to learn anything—cultural literacy or basics—requires an engagement of the mind.

Since change and growth are viewed as intellectual processes, not events, we are interested in and value the time invested in ownership, commitment, and long-range learning.

6. Tangible Support

Like radio transmitters, how school personnel expend their valuable resources—time, energy, and money—sets up a signal system to the staff, community, and students about what is important.

Financial resources are allocated to hire substitutes so that teachers can be released to visit and coach each other. Staff members and parents are sent to workshops, courses, conferences, and other inservice opportunities to learn more about effective thinking and the teaching of thinking.

Administrators use their time and energy to visit classrooms to learn more about and coach instruction in thinking. Teachers expend their valuable time in planning lessons and observing each other teach for thinking. Time in the classroom is allocated to thinking and talking about thinking. The processes of thinking are explicitly stated so that students know that learning to think is the goal of the lesson. Problem solving and metacognition *are* the "tasks that students are on."

7. Caring, Celebrations, Humor

The value of thinking is exemplified in the traditions, celebrations, and humorous events that indicate thoughtful behavior is being achieved.

Staff members may be heard sharing humorous anecdotes of students' thought processes. ("I observed two seventh grade boys on the athletic field yesterday. From their behavior, I could tell a scuffle was about to break out.

Before I got to them, another boy intervened and I overheard him say, 'Hey, you guys, restrain your impulsivity'").

Teachers and administrators share personal, humorous, and sometimes embarrassing anecdotes of their own lack of thinking. (Tactics for remembering peoples' names, strategies for finding their car in the parking lot, or creative solutions to the dilemma of locking their keys in the car.)

At school assemblies students and teachers are honored for acts of creativity, cooperation, thoughtfulness, innovation, and scholarly accomplishments. Academic decathlons, thinking fairs, problem-solving tournaments, dialogical debates, invention conventions, science fairs, art exhibitions, and musical programs celebrate the benefits of strategic planning, careful research, practice, creativity, and cooperation.

Career days are held in which local business and industry leaders describe what reasoning, creative problem solving, and cooperative skills are needed in various jobs and occupations.

8. Communications

Thinking skills pervade all forms of communication from and within the school. Report cards, parent conferences, and other forms of progress reports include indicators of students' growth of intelligent behaviors. (Asking questions, metacognition, flexibility of thinking, persistence, listening to others' points of view, creativity, etc.) (Costa 1984).

Portfolios of students' work are collected over time as sources of data about growth in organizational abilities, conceptual development, and increased creativity. Test scores are reported that include reasoning, vocabulary growth, critical thinking, analogies, problem solving, and fluency. Parent education meetings are held to help parents know how to enhance their child's intelligent behavior (Feldman 1984).

Newspaper articles are written, calendars and newsletters are sent home informing parents and the community of the school's intent and progress in teaching thinking (Diamandis and Obermark 1986-87). In parent meetings suggestions are given for ways to enhance their children's intellectual capacities.

Students maintain journals to record their own thinking and metacognition and to share and compare their growth of insight, creativity, and problem-solving strategies over time. Parents, too, are invited to collect evidence of transference of their child's intellectual growth from the classroom to family and home situations.

9. *Continuing To Expand The Knowledge Base*

The mark of a school that is becoming a home for the mind is that it is continually expanding the knowledge base instead of striving for conformity to certain specified instructional competencies. Knowledge about thinking and the teaching of thinking is vast, complex, uncertain and incomplete (Marzano, et al. 1987). No one will ever know it all nor do we wish to reduce it to a simplistic step-by-step lesson plan (Brandt 1987). Teachers and administrators can continually learn more and add to their repertoire of instructional skills and strategies.

Knowing that the school's mission is to develop the intellect and that process is valued as much as content, each teacher at each grade level and within each subject area will strive to invest thoughtful learning, reflection, and metacognition into all instruction. Teachers constantly expand their repertoire of instructional skills and strategies intended to develop in students a wide range of reasoning, creative, and cooperative abilities. They strive to match their instructional behaviors, tactics, and strategies from this vast repertoire with content goals, students' characteristics, and context with which they are working. They vary their lesson designs according to students' developmental levels, cognitive styles, and modality preferences (Jones 1987).

Teachers and administrators take course work in philosophy, logic, and critical thinking and strive to improve their own thinking skills and strategies while their students expand their range of intelligent behaviors. These include not only knowing how to perform specific thought processes (Beyer 1986), but also knowing what to do when solutions to problems are *not* immediately known—study skills, learning to learn, reasoning, problem-solving, and decision-making strategies (Marzano and Arredondo 1986). They learn about their own cognitive styles and how to be cooperative with others who have differing styles. They learn how to cause their own "creative juices" to flow by brainstorming, inventing metaphor, synectics, and concept mapping.

observers are invited to give feedback about the group's effectiveness and growth in their decision-making, consensus-seeking, and communication skills.

Furthermore, each group member's opinions are respected. Disagreements can be stated without fear of damaging the relationship. Debates and alternate points of view are encouraged. Responsibility for "errors, omissions, and inadequacies" is owned without blaming others. Responses are given and justified and new ideas are advanced without fear of being criticized or judged. Differing priorities, values, logic, and philosophical beliefs of group members are discussed and become the topics of analysis, dialogue, and understanding.

10. Trust, Honesty, And Open Communication

All the school's inhabitants are committed to the improvement of school climate, interpersonal relationships, and the quality of human interaction. Students and classified and certificated personnel strive for precision of language, understanding, and empathy. They practice and improve their listening skills of paraphrasing, empathizing, and clarifying.

At school board, administrative, faculty, and class meetings decision-making processes are discussed, explicated, and adopted. Process

11. Philosophy, Policies, And Practices

Enhancing intelligent behavior is explicitly stated in the school district's adopted philosophy and mission. District policies and practices are constantly scrutinized for their consistency with and contribution to that philosophy. Evidence of their use as criteria for decision making is examined. Furthermore, procedures for continuing to study, refine, and improve district-wide practices are aligned so that schools keep growing toward more thoughtful practice.

Personnel practices reflect the desire to infuse thinking. Job specifications for hiring new personnel include skills in teaching thinking. Teachers are empowered to make decisions that affect them—they have a sense of efficacy. Supervision of, and staff development for, all certificated staff are focused on enhancing their perceptions and intellectual growth and honors their role as professional decision makers (Costa and Garmston 1985).

Selection criteria for texts, tests, instructional materials and other media include their contribution to thinking. Counseling and discipline, library, and psychological services are constantly evaluated for their enhancement of and consistency with thoughtful practice.

In schools and classrooms discipline practices appeal to students' thoughtful behavior. Students participate in generating rational and compassionate classroom and school rules and are involved in evaluating their own behavior in relation to those criteria.

metacognitive strategies in the presence of students and others while they are teaching, planning, and problem solving (Jones 1987).

Staff members restrain their impulsivity during emotional crises. They listen to students, parents, and each other with empathy, precision, and understanding. Teachers and administrators constantly reflect on and evaluate their own behaviors and strive to make them more consistent with the core value and belief that thoughtful behavior is a valid goal of education.

In Summary

The school will become a home for the mind only when the total school is an intellectually stimulating environment for all the participants; when all the school's inhabitants realize that freeing human intellectual potential is the goal of education; when they strive to get better at it themselves; and when they use their energies to enhance the intelligent behaviors of others.

12. Modeling

Learning to think is probably best learned through imitation and emulation of significant others. All adults in the school, therefore, strive to model in their own behaviors those same qualities and behaviors that are desired in students.

Modeling will be evident as teachers and administrators share their

References

Adler, M. *The Paideia Proposal.* New York: Macmillan, 1982.

Beyer, B. "Teaching Critical Thinking: A Direct Approach." *Social Education,* 49 (1985), 297-303.

Bloom, A. *The Closing Of The American Mind*. New York: Simon and Schuster, 1987.

Brandt, R. "On Teaching Thinking Skills: A Conversation with B. Othanel Smith." Alexandria, VA: *Educational Leadership*. October, 1987. Vol 45, No. 2.

Costa, A. "Teacher Behaviors that Enhance Thinking." In *Developing Minds: A Resource Book For Teaching Thinking*. Ed. A. Costa. Alexandria, VA: Association for Supervision and Curriculum Development, 1984a.

Costa, A. "How Can We Recognize Improved Student Thinking?" In *Developing Minds: A Resource Book For Teaching Thinking*. Ed. A. Costa. Alexandria, VA: Association for Supervision and Curriculum Development, 1984b.

Costa, A. and Garmston, R. "Supervision for Intelligent Teaching." *Educational Leadership*, p. 70-80, February, 1985.

Deal, T. Presentation made at the National ASCD Convention, New Orleans, LA, 1987.

Diamandis, L. and Obermark, C. "Bright Ideas—A Newsletter For Parents: Critical Thinking Activities For Kindergarten Children." Sorento, IL.

Feldman, R.D. "How to Improve your Child's Intelligent Behavior." *Women's Day*, November 11, 1986.

Hirsch, E.D. *Cultural Literacy*. Boston, MA: Houghton Mifflin, 1987.

Jones, B.F. "Strategic Teaching: A Cognitive Focus." In B.F. Jones, A.S. Palincsar, D. Ogle, and E. Carr. (Eds.) *Strategic Teaching And Learning: Cognitive Instruction In The Content Areas*. Alexandria, VA: Association for Supervision and Curriculum Development, 1987.

Kohn, A. "Art for Art's Sake." *Psychology Today*. September, 1987, Vol 21, No. 9, p. 52-57.

MacLean, P. "A Mind of Three Minds: Educating the Triune Brain." In J. Chall and A. Mirsky (Eds.) *Education And The Brain. Seventy-Seventh Yearbook of the National Society for the Study of Education*. Chicago: University of Chicago Press, 1978.

Marzano, R. and Arredondo, D. *Tactics For Thinking*. Alexandria, VA: Association for Supervision and Curriculum Development, 1986.

Marzano, R.; Brandt, R.; Hughes, C.; Jones, B. F.; Presseisen, B.; Rankin, S.; and Suhor, C. *Dimensions Of Thinking*. Alexandria VA: Association for Supervision and Curriculum Development, 1987.

Pascarella, P. *The New Achievers*. New York, NY: Free Press, 1984.

Perkins, D. *The Mind's Best Work: A New Psychology Of Creative Thinking*. Cambridge, MA: Harvard University Press, 1983.

Ravich, D. and Finn, C. *What Do Our 17 Year Olds Know?* New York: Harper and Row, 1987.

Saphier, J. Presentation made at the Annual ASCD Convention, New Orleans, LA., 1987.

Vygotsky, L. *Society of Mind.* Cambridge, MA: Harvard University Press, 1978.

I wish to thank Jon Saphier and Terence Deal. They identified these norms as being characteristic of schools and institutions which keep improving. I also wish to thank Bob Garmston of California State University, Sacramento; Becky Van der Bogart, Assistant Superintendent, Groton-Dunstable School District, Groton, Massachusetts; Ed Barbari, Principal, Westover School, Stamford, Connecticut; and Marilyn Tabor, Mentor Teacher, Irvine Unified School District, Irvine, California for contributing their helpful suggestions and for confirming these indicators as workable and valid indicators of infusion of thinking skills.

--------------- ‿‿ ---------------

Section V
The School As A Home
For The Mind: The Re-vision

"We are riding the crest
of what may well be the greatest
opportunity for educational reform in
history; a growing dissatisfaction with the
current quality of education; a realization
of educational reform as a political
platform; a heightened awareness of the
demands of an uncertain future; a concern
about our nation's global economic
dependence upon an educated and highly
skilled work force; and face-to-face
encounters with our delicate ecological
home...Let us unite in common voice. If
we desire our future world to be more
compassionate, more cooperative, and
more thoughtful, we must work together to
make it happen... Mindworkers unite."
—*Arthur L. Costa*

M ind Workers Unite!

F rom visits to many "thinking schools," and from dialogues with school personnel embarking on "Phase II" of their cognitive curriculum transformations (the "beyond awareness" stage), I have become keenly aware of some unfinished tasks for those interested in pursuing, sustaining, and expanding curriculum and instruction intended to develop students' intellectual powers.

The metaphor I choose to describe this task is *orchestration.* It is a fitting metaphor because it engenders a vision of precision and harmony working diligently together toward a common goal, and, ultimately, producing beautiful music. I propose seven next steps in the orchestration process: definition, integration, application, articulation, individualization, politicization, and evaluation. Obviously, there are many schools which have taken these steps; others are not yet concerned with them. These are merely suggestions from one person's point of view.

Each member of a staff is an extremely talented professional. The third grade teacher may be similar to an outstanding "violinist." The high school history teacher is like a master "cellist." The middle school industrial arts teacher is comparable to a marvelous "flutist" and so on. Each, in their own right, is an expert. (The Italian word for teacher is *"maestro."*)

In an orchestra, however, musicians play in the same key, and at the same tempo. They rehearse together and have a common vision of the entire score, each knowing well the part they play that contributes to the whole. They do not all play at the same time; there are rests, harmonies, fugues, and counterpoint. They support each other in a totally coordinated and concerted effort. In the same way, teachers can support each other in creating an overall curriculum. They neither teach the same thinking processes at the same time, nor do they approach them in the same way. Their cumulative effect, however, is beautiful, harmonious "music" in the mind and learning of the student.

1. Definition:

Our first task of orchestration is to decide on and to be able to communicate our definitions and outcomes of instruction.

If you ask almost any individual school member to define "thinking," you'll get about as many definitions as there are staff members. The positive effects in those districts that have forged a common definition of thinking, however, are becoming increasingly apparent. Not that all schools have the same definition; rather, a school staff shares a common vision. They can describe the attributes of the ideal thinking person; whether it be characteristics of the "critical thinker"; dispositions of intelligent human beings; qualities of the "thought-full" person; or performances of efficient, effective, and reasoned problem solvers; the name is not as important as the shared meaning and vision these terms convey.

2. Integration:

The struggle to infuse thinking into curriculum content areas, instruction, and school climate continues.

Limitations of time and communication in school settings often prevent teachers from different departments, grade levels, and disciplines from meeting together. The mutual support, continuity, reinforcement, and transference of thinking skills throughout the grade levels and across the subject areas has yet to be accomplished. "Critical reading," the "scientific method," "problem solving" in mathematics, literacy, and numeracy, "modes of inquiry," study skills.... The distinctions and connections are still vague when deciding which should be taught in science, which are most appropriate to math, which should be included in the social sciences, and how they all fit together.

Until we consider thinking as the core of the curriculum and until content is selectively abandoned or judiciously included because of its contributions to the thinking/learning process, we shall continue to endure this dilemma. The sooner we admit that the process *is* the content, the sooner we will find ways to infuse thinking across the curriculum. Our obsession with content is what separates us.

Rather than including science or math or the arts in the curriculum as ends in themselves, we will ask, what is the unique nature, structure, and modes of inquiry that can be drawn from each of these disciplines to be learned and applied elsewhere. As we make this fundamental shift, our instruction will also be altered. We will change our view from learning *of* the content, to learning *from* the content. We will refocus from mastering content

164

and concepts as an end, to the application of knowledge, the transference of cognitive strategies, and the tackling with confidence of new problems that command increasingly complex reasoning, more intricate logic and more imaginative and creative solutions.

But thinking is not just for students. It must be infused into the total culture of the school. Teachers will more likely teach for thinking if they are in an intellectually stimulating environment themselves. Schools are increasingly employing practices which signal the school's real values: focusing on teaching as decision making; staff development intended to engage and enhance teacher's intellect; providing numerous opportunities for teachers to strengthen their collaborative problem-solving and decision-making abilities; and encouraging risk-taking, creativity, and experimentation. To integrate thinking into the school culture may also require "purging" some school practices which detract from the central goal of thinking: discipline techniques or teacher evaluation practices, for example (Costa 1991).

Such practices and policies send a powerful signal to the staff and the community that thinking is not just "kid's stuff." Thinking will be integrated when it pervades all subject areas, is the central purpose of instruction, and is reflected in the policies and practices governing all the school's inhabitants.

3. Application:

Recent results of the National Assessment of Educational Progress (Lapointe 1991) indicate that while our students are improving in their basic skills, they still seem unable to apply reasoning and critical thinking skills in new and novel situations.

For transference of learning to become a reality, teachers will need to meet together to plan opportunities for bridging, revisiting, and generalizing concepts and processes. They will need to systematically collect evidence of transference across subject areas. Thematic, trans-disciplinary instruction strategically designed to have students encounter similar problems and to apply analogous problem-solving strategies in increasingly more "distant" settings, and deliberately teaching for transfer by scaffolding and bridging can habituate the students' inclination to draw forth from previous experience and apply it to new and novel situations. (Perkins and Salomon 1990)

4. Articulation:

Over time, as students progress through the grades, their problem solving will build toward more complexity, greater abstractness, and increased creativity. This will necessitate a vertical coherence of the curriculum as well as the cross disciplinary, horizontal integration described in 2 above.

Many examples of repetitive curriculum can be cited. Ask a district faculty where, for example, fractions are taught. You may find they are introduced, practiced, reviewed, and retaught at almost every grade level through high school. Articulation further requires attention to students' developmental needs. Students will require less repetition when concepts and processes are taught at developmentally appropriate levels, employing all the senses, and in a manner which engages and transforms the mind.

5. *Individualization:*

One of the great benefits of cognitive education is that it is so all-encompassing. Under this broad umbrella, there is room for creative and critical thinking, convergent and divergent thinking, precision and intuition, induction and deduction, metacognition and meditation, visualization, listening and language production. There is no one way to think; rather, all of these intellectual capacities are valued and the broader the range we acquire, the more efficient problem solvers we become.

Human beings strive to be unique. We differ in our modality preferences, styles, culture, background of information, and early childhood rearing. We have different signatures and different fingerprints; we even emit unique vibration rates from the aura surrounding our bodies.

We place great value on athletes and recognize differences in their abilities. We appreciate the gracefulness of the lithe ballerina, the huskiness of the burly wrestler, the alertness of the swift quarterback, the speed of the lanky sprinter, the control of the diver, the stamina of the marathoner, and the agility of the ice skater. Seldom, however, do we find an athlete who excels in *all* sports. Individual disposition, skeletal structure, musculature, and perceptual abilities both place limits upon and enhance each athlete's performance.

Likewise, we know that each of us has an individual cognitive style that determines how we perceive and act upon our world. Like athletics, the teaching of thinking can help students celebrate their own unique "style" and genetic makeup, and to understand the effects of their individuality on their perceptions and thinking processes. We can assist them in respecting and preserving the uniqueness of others who possess and display different styles, and we can help them continue to add to their repertoire of styles and strategies.

6. *Politicization:*

As a goal of education, the development of the intellect is not yet valued or understood by the majority of the public. While business and industry leaders are becoming increasingly supportive of the school's endeavor to educate the future generation to

166

become better individual and group problem solvers, to develop their creative capacities, to be open to new and continued learning, and to work cooperatively as a member of a team, there are still legislators, governors, school boards, and even an "Education President" who fail to include thinking in our national goals for the twenty-first century.

Educators, in conjunction with test makers, textbook publishers, business and industry leaders, and the media, need to mount a massive information and educational program intended to shift public policy and national values toward support of a more rational, cooperative, and compassionate mission statement for public education.

7. Evaluation:

You cannot measure performance of process-oriented goals using product-oriented evaluations. How to organize a meaningful, systematic, rigorous assessment program and how to find ways of communicating results to parents, school boards, and the various publics still befuddles many educators. While we believe in authentic assessments—keeping portfolios, extended projects, interviews, journals, and the like—we must still transform the public's understanding of these procedures, all of which are quite contrary to their past experience and diet of college entrance exams, achievement tests, rank-ordered school ratings in the local newspapers based on gain scores,

intelligence quotients, and qualification for gifted or Chapter I programs.

My greatest worry about cognitive education, however, is that we will become complacent about our achievements. We have a history of being swept along by fads and bandwagons. I fear that groups will say, "Thinking skills? We tried that last year, and it didn't work." Any change takes time, energy, and devotion. We are deeply into the awareness stage of reform. Historical research on educational change effort indicates that many innovations were not fully realized because they were abandoned prematurely without institutionalizing the change (Hall and Hord 1987).

We are riding the crest of what may well be the greatest opportunity for educational reform in history: a growing dissatisfaction with the current quality of education; a realization of educational reform as a political platform; a heightened awareness of the demands of an uncertain future; a concern about our nations' global economic dependence upon an educated and highly skilled work force; and face-to-face encounters with our delicate ecological home.

Do not relent; don't give up in the face of adversity. One of the greatest of intelligent behaviors is persistence. Let us unite into a common voice. If we desire our future world to be more compassionate, more cooperative and more thoughtful, we must work together to make it happen.

References

Costa, A. "The School as a Home for the Mind." In A. L. Costa (Ed.), *Developing Minds.* Alexandria, VA: Association for Supervision and Curriculum Development, 1991.

Hall, G. E. and Hord, S. M. *Change in Schools, Facilitating the Process.* Albany, NY: State University of New York Press, 1987.

Lapointe, A. "A Summary of Findings from the Nation's Report Card." In A. L. Costa (Ed.), *Developing Minds.* Alexandria, VA: Association for Supervision and Curriculum Development, 1991.

Perkins, D. N. and Salomon, G. "Teaching for Transfer." In A. L. Costa (Ed.), *Developing Minds.* Alexandria, VA: Association for Supervision and Curriculum Development, 1991.

———— ࠤ ————

Index

A

Accommodation, 45-46, 97, 105
Accuracy
  checking, 145
  striving, 24-25
Action research, as indicator of thinking
  skills infusion, 151
Adams, Marilyn J., 26-27
Addition, as linguistic cue, 117
Administrator, role of, in enhancing
  thinking skills, 129-135
Aesthetics
  definition of, 17
  importance of, in cognitive education,
  17-18
Anecdotes, 12
Appreciation, 11-12
  as indicator of thinking skills infusion,
  151-152
Articulation, in orchestration process, 165-
  166

B

Behavioral objective statements, verbs that
  serve as predicates, 47, 48-49
Brain functioning, 11, 36-37, 45-46
Brandt, Ron, 35

C

Career days, 12

Caring, 12, 154
Categorizing, sample lesson for teaching,
  79-82
Causality, as linguistic cue, 117
Celebrations, 12
  as indicator of thinking skills infusion,
  154
Child-study teams, 10
Choices, conscious, to enhance
  metacognition, 90-91
Clarification, as teacher response behavior,
  62-63
Classification, sample lesson for teaching,
  79-82
Classroom clues, teacher's use, 102-104
Classroom management, language used in,
  112
Classroom time, to teach thinking, 70
Cogitare
  avoiding negative presuppositions,
  115-116
  classroom management, 112
  discipline, 111-112
  metacognition, 114-115
  probing for specificity, 113-114
  providing data, not solutions, 112
  speaking, 109-110
  studying, 117
  thinking words, 110
Cognitive autonomy, as goal in cognitive
  coaching, 123
Cognitive coaching
  assumptions, 121-122
  coaching competencies, 123-124

169

T